Dear Reader:

You hold in your hand the result of many years of effort by many people who began by asking the simple question, "What does a church really do?" That may sound like a simple question but you might be surprised at the responses I have heard for the past ten years.

What *does* a church really do to obey the Lord and fulfill the Great Commission? You and I know that there are a million methods, models, and manuals describing church practices but where can we find out what a church really does?

I think you will find answers in this book to help you understand what a church really does and whether or not your church is currently doing what it takes to be a kingdom focused church. This is not a book filled with theory or practice. What you will find inside is a biblical view of what a church is and what it does successfully. You will find help to analyze, repurpose and even celebrate your church's ministry and your own ministry.

I hope you accept this complimentary copy of *The Kingdom Focused Church* as a gift from me with the hope that you and your people will live your lives a fullest capacity as you further God's great kingdom. If you enjoy what you read please recommend it to others who can benefit from it also.

Gene Mims
LifeWay Christian Resources
April, 2003

THE
KINGDOM
FOCUSED
CHURCH

THE
KINGDOM
FOCUSED
CHURCH

A COMPELLING IMAGE OF AN ACHIEVABLE
FUTURE FOR YOUR CHURCH

GENE MIMS

BROADMAN
&HOLMAN
PUBLISHERS

NASHVILLE, TENNESSEE

Special limited edition. Not for resale.
For purchases, request ISBN 0-8054-2080-0

Published by Broadman & Holman Publishers
Nashville, Tennessee

Dewey Decimal Classification: 262.7
Subject Heading: CHURCH-BIBLICAL TEACHING \
CHURCH RENEWAL \ KINGDOM OF GOD

Psalms, Proverbs, and New Testament Scripture quotations are
taken from the Holman Christian Standard Bible, © Copyright
2000 by Holman Bible Publishers. Used by permission. Other Old
Testament Scripture quotations are taken from the Holy Bible, *New
International Version,* copyright © 1973, 1978, 1984 by
International Bible Society.

1 2 3 4 5 6 7 8 9 10 08 07 06 05 04 03

Contents

PREFACE

I AM STRUGGLING TO WRITE THESE WORDS as my eyes drift to a serene setting in the mountains of North Carolina. My wife and I are spending a few days in a mountain cabin tucked away from the frenetic pace of Nashville. I thought by coming here I would be able to write with ease, but it is not to be. I am constantly tempted to look out the windows at the scenery or stop to listen to the birds as they call to each other.

But the surroundings are not my only struggle in writing these words. I am deeply troubled by what I have observed over the past years in churches I have pastored, attended, helped as a transitional pastor, served as a consultant, and heard about from friends. It seems to me that as the pace of change increases around the world and certainly in the United States, churches, pastors, leaders, and experts strain to find the right understandings and combinations to help the local churches fulfill the Great Commission and build the lives of believers in those congregations.

Let's face it, church is a hard, exciting, and often confusing place to be these days. I say this with deep affection and high esteem for churches and pastors. I do not intend to be numbered with the increasing hoard of people who find comfort and make a living from church bashing. Most of those folks either have little experience in successful church leadership or they have deep, unresolved spiritual issues.

Having said that, I think we can do better in this age of fast change. But this is not a book about change. It is not a book about methods or techniques. It will not answer all the questions you may have about worship, preaching, discipleship, or small groups. This is a book about focus and more specifically *kingdom focus.* I believe that many of our churches and many of our leaders are out of focus.

I do not mean that leaders are out of touch. Most leaders live at the crossroads of life with their people, observing all sorts of dilemmas, struggles, victories, joys, and griefs. I do not think leaders lack calling or character. Despite a few exceptions, most pastors and church leaders I know are truly called and display pristine character. I do not think the problem is methodology or style. Most leaders I know are creative, well-informed, and solid people.

I believe the problem is *focus.* If we lack a kingdom focus in our work, it shows up everywhere. While we are active at an unprecedented level, our results are not what we expect. We have more methodologies, styles, small groups, conferences, resources, and programs than ever before, but we lack a foundational focus.

This lack of focus does not mean that there is a lack of intention. On the contrary, I see great intentions, great dreams, great plans, and great displays of courage and stamina. But many of our leaders and their churches are out of focus, and we are paying a high price for it.

Jesus Christ came to earth to fulfill the work of the Father in saving people from their sin. He came to live His life and to give His life in order that we might have salvation and live abundant lives. He left a church that He called into being to fulfill what He began on earth. He gave believers a Great Commission so that we might always know what to do. He left no doubt about *what to do,* but He left the *how to* in our hands. Every church and every pastor I know realizes the importance of the Great Commission. It is the grand statement of Christianity and forever stands above time and place.

But the Great Commission is not the focus of our lives and work. It was not the focus of the life of Christ. Nor was church growth, discipleship, evangelism, ministry, preaching, or teaching. While all of these are crucial to fulfilling the Great Commission, His focus was on one thing—*the kingdom of God!*

I want to hasten to add here that the kingdom of God is not a necessary ingredient to add to the other things noted above. It is *the necessary ingredient* to which we add the Great Commission, evangelism, discipleship, fellowship, ministry, and worship. All the good things we do in church make sense only in light of the kingdom of God.

The kingdom of God is the reign of God in today's world. The kingdom is the ultimate reality and sovereign movement of God in the universe. This is expressed in the transforming truth that Jesus Christ rules over all things and is evidenced by God's supernatural work in and through believers in local churches. The kingdom of God must be the central life focus that every person should seek and align with in order to know the full and abundant life God created people to experience in Christ.

If we could see our churches as a crucial part of God's work in the universe today, it would change much of what we do (and don't do) and give us confidence and direction. We need a kingdom focus to meet the challenges of a fast-changing world. We need a kingdom focus to understand our world and its movements. Without a kingdom focus, we flounder from program to program, from disappointment to disappointment, and from one fad to another. In the meantime, our churches are suffering and people are overcome with sin and spiritual struggles.

We should agree that a church is a kingdom community of believers gathered locally in dynamic fellowship under Christ's lordship. That community has a purpose; it fills the most important kingdom role of any institution on earth. Nothing is greater than the kingdom of God, and nothing is more important to the kingdom on earth than the church. Because of this, pastors and churches are crucial to kingdom work.

With a kingdom focus, any church can and will flourish. A kingdom-focused church will be strong in times of trouble and change. It will be certain in uncertain times. It will persevere with confidence in God's work. It will thrive when neighborhoods fail and circumstances turn bad. A kingdom-focused church is a powerful tool the Lord uses to accomplish His purposes.

If what I've said is true, and it is, why is it then that our churches are not flourishing, are not certain or thriving in difficult times? The answer lies above all in developing a kingdom focus.

Chapter 1

IN SEARCH OF THE
PERFECT CHURCH

MIKE IS ONE OF A NUMBER of rising stars in the world of pastors and churches. He has been effective for several years, and the church he now pastors has great possibilities. In fact, the church's growth is so great that he is finding it hard to keep up with what is happening. When he first started out with a smaller church, he struggled to manage his time and lack of resources. He always thought that the Lord's blessings and success would make his life much easier, but somehow that has not happened.

Mike is fully committed to his call and work. He loves his people and is eager to do whatever it takes to see them grow in the Lord and to serve Him. But lately he has begun to feel a pressure that he doesn't quite understand. He can't seem to find the time to get on top of everything. His daily plans always seem to get sidetracked with unforeseen interruptions and crises. He is very much aware that his family time is suffering, and he feels pulled in two directions.

It's Monday morning, and Mike sits in his study. He is tired from yesterday. Preaching, spending time with the folks, two important committee meetings, and a quick visit to the hospital would wear anyone down. On top of that, he had a wedding Saturday, complete with a rehearsal Friday night. There was just enough time left for his son Sam's soccer match and daughter Jennifer's first T-ball game.

Days like this are not easy to handle because this week's calendar looks just as full. If his personal calendar is not enough of a nightmare, then the church calendar would be. Put the two together, and Mike has a disaster brewing.

Mike is not living an unusual life for a pastor. He is beginning a common experience that represents a crossroads for him. He doesn't know it, but the next few months will likely determine his and his congregation's spiritual health and effectiveness over the next ten years.

Mike *can* choose to do many things, but the one thing he *must* do is to find the right focus for himself and his church. He faces a plethora of activities, ministries, opportunities, and challenges. Every pastor and every church face the same issues. What most also have in common is a lack of focus that negates effective spiritual transformation of believers and their ministries.

As he sits at his desk wondering about his life, his future, and his true effectiveness, his mind turns to a dangerous notion—but one he thinks of often. Mike wonders if the church that recently contacted him might just be the perfect church for him. Just maybe, he reasons, this could be the turning point. This could be the place. The perfect church would surely let him rise to his fullest potential. *The perfect church* . . . .

If you're a pastor, or if you're a church member who has given a lot of thought and prayer to what your church ought to be, you, too, have a vision of "the perfect church." Of course, everybody's perfect church is a little different. Some meet in huge auditoriums, while others worship in picturesque wooden chapels. One has enormous impact in the neighborhood, and another supports an army of foreign missionaries in every corner of the world. One brings in contemporary Christian music stars, and another has the finest pipe organ money can buy.

No matter how different they are on the surface, perfect churches share a number of key characteristics. They're filled with people on fire for Christ who put selfishness, politics, and personal agendas aside to the glory of God and His chosen purpose. They treat their pastors with respect and pay them fairly. They give generously, evangelize tirelessly, and teach truthfully. They are a joy and a blessing to every member and visitor and a shining beacon in the communities they so faithfully serve.

And all perfect churches have one more thing in common. They don't exist.

We may as well face the facts right up front: there is no such thing as a perfect church. "But wait," you say with an indulgent smile, "I know where there's a perfect church!" However, the perfect church you're thinking about is invariably the one you're about to join, or the one you're looking for, or the one you belonged to when you were a child. It's the one where you were married years ago or the one you and some Christian friends are getting ready to start next summer as soon as school is out.

The perfect church is a figment of your imagination and mine, an idealized vision that requires unachievable standards of harmony and singleness of mind. And if by some miracle we were actually to stumble upon the perfect church and join it, then it wouldn't be perfect anymore because we'd be members and we're not perfect!

Every church is imperfect because it's made up of imperfect people, and they will produce imperfect results. It's been that way since the beginning. Paul reminded the Ephesians that the church was the bride of Christ but that they'd better watch what they were thinking. The ancient church in Corinth had deep immorality within its ranks, and the church in Thessalonica had members who wouldn't lift a finger in service to the Christian cause.

Sound familiar?

The church isn't a fortress in the community but a wide-open door through which people come with all their culture, prejudice, sin, hang-ups, background, and baggage elbowing in along with them. Church members bring their sinful nature into the church the same way they bring it into the bank or the grocery store. Sinners and their sin are inseparable. We may be on our best behavior in God's house, but at one time or another, all of us will have our sinfulness boil to the surface.

And so the church—your church—is where a deacon might elope with the receptionist, or the student minister has an affair with that beautiful blond alto in the third row. Couples get divorced, kids get pregnant, and embezzlers get three-to-five. It's where life happens. It's also where faith is enriched and forgiveness is asked and bestowed. It's where people come in spite of their sin to claim the power of Christ in their lives. If nobody ever sinned, nobody would ever need the church.

There's a dramatic difference between the church of the kingdom, which *is* perfect, and the local church, which is a mess. Maybe that's why, over more than thirty years as a pastor, I've spent so much time focusing on the church I *didn't* have. I was hoping sooner or later I'd have the chance to build a church exactly in line with the kingdom ideal—if people would just get out of my way and let me do it!

I see pastors across the world almost every day, many of them young and full of promise, who are so frustrated with their work and so discouraged. They're trying to build the perfect kingdom church with imperfect worldly materials (including themselves), and they can't figure out why it doesn't work. They stew over what they ought to change—maybe the preaching style or the old-timers on the worship committee.

Let's go back for a moment to our dedicated, yet frazzled, friend Pastor Mike. He reads books and goes to seminars and surfs the Internet looking frantically for answers. Nothing seems like an obvious solution, but finally he picks a couple of new ideas and tries them out. Nobody likes the changes, and, what's worse, the service is ten minutes longer now and the Presbyterians are beating everybody to the cafeteria at the mall. So Mike tries something else, only half-heartedly this time because he doesn't really believe in this particular new wrinkle himself. He just thinks anything will be better than sticking with the dreary old status quo.

Too often Mike and his fellow pastors lose their direction in a snowstorm of advice, programs, paradigms, conflicting goals, burnout, and despair. They end up trapped in a whiteout, powerless and without any sense of direction. Is it their own fault? Are they simply not cut out to lead a church? Should they hightail it over to the community college and sign up for some real estate courses?

Of course not. What they really need to do is recognize and understand a few basics about the essential nature of the church— ideas so simple they're easy to overlook, and so big they can transform a weary and dispirited pastor into a powerful and effective leader of his congregation.

First, as we've already seen, *no church is perfect*. If you're looking for one, you're looking for something that doesn't exist this side of heaven. Certainly every church and every pastor should work hard to be as perfect as possible. In saying no church is perfect, no one is giving you permission to slack off and say, "Oh well, we're all a bunch of sinners, and this is the best we can do."

If we were perfect, we wouldn't need a church; but we aren't, so we do. And we need churches now more than ever. Over the past generation families and communities have been fragmented as never before in our history. The relatives and neighbors who once supported ministers aren't there like they used to be. Epidemic levels of divorce and illegitimacy feed the fires of cultural instability and uncertainty that threaten the present and darken our future.

People need something to believe in—something that's bigger than themselves. And if the church doesn't reach out with the message that Christ loves them and died for them, their spiritual longing will be answered with the heresy of New Age ideas, the occult, Islam, Mormonism, or some other false religion. If people don't know about the true God, they'll make do with something else.

In short, the sinfulness that keeps your church from being the perfect church is the same sinfulness that makes it essential for you not to give up but to keep pastoring, serving, building, and improving the imperfect church you have.

A second basic idea about the church is that *the only church you can change is the one you're serving in right now.* You can't develop an effective plan for improving the church you have if you're also hard at work on your exit strategy, pining away for the church of your imagination, or wishing for the one you left ten years ago.

This means you have to avoid the temptation to say, "You know, the church is supposed to be . . ." or "I need to be in a church that . . . ." I have to admit I've said those things myself a few times over the years. "I thought the church was supposed to be a place where people got along!" Well it's supposed to be that, but it isn't always. Conflicts, opinions, and hidden agendas fester on every pew, and the pastor is charged with the responsibility of somehow moving forward in spite of them.

Your church isn't the church you want; it's the church you have. It isn't the idyllic church of next summer or last year but the church of the here and now. Furthermore, your church isn't Saddleback and it isn't Willow Creek. These are just two of a number of large, prominent, high-impact churches that many pastors look at longingly (perhaps even enviously) and say, "Wow! We need to be like those guys! Look how successful they are! Let's adopt their worship style, their outreach programs, their publicity." They eagerly snap up and devour the excellent books by Bill Hybels about Willow Creek and Rick Warren about Saddleback, poring over them for solutions to their own stagnating ministries.

What these well-meaning pastors forget, though, is that most of them aren't in southern California, where Saddleback is, or in suburban Chicago, home of Willow Creek. They have an entirely different set of needs, gifts, resources, opportunities, expectations, and limitations to work with. If God wanted them to replicate Saddleback or Willow Creek (or Woodstock, or any other dynamic, influential, high-profile church), He would have given them what He gave the members and leaders of those famous congregations.

God gave those people one set of tools, and they did the best they could with them. Your job isn't to whine that God gave you different tools but to build absolutely the best church possible with the tools you have. Theodore Roosevelt—military hero, conservationist, steadfast Christian, and the youngest man ever to serve as president of the United States—summed it up best by advising, "Do what you can, with what you have, where you are."

The third basic point about the church brings us to the reason for this book in the first place: *every successful church is a kingdom-focused church.* Congregations flounder and pastors suffer vocational crashes because they're trying to concentrate on something (or a lot of somethings) other than the kingdom of God.

The misdirected focus that cripples so many congregations isn't the result of laziness, incompetence, or malice. Church leaders and members for the most part work hard and pray sincerely for their church, but they get sidetracked, distracted. Their attention becomes divided among a variety of goals; their resources get parceled out to a growing number of ministries. And in the end, by trying to go in every direction at once, they don't go anywhere at all.

Have you heard this before? Perhaps experienced it yourself, as I surely have? When the church doesn't know where it's going, it has no way to judge whether any particular ministry or program will help it get there. Does somebody have a heart for inner-city ministries? Then start an inner-city ministry! Does the youth minister love Mexico? Then send the youth to Mexico! Anyone with a good story and the ear of the finance committee can get a ministry going. But to what end? *Why?* If you don't know where you're going, you have no idea whether you're headed in the right direction. You can't tell whether a ministry is strengthening or weakening your church. If you do not have the right goal, you will hit your target—failure— every time!

In the Model Prayer, Jesus taught us to pray, "Your kingdom come. Your will be done on earth as it is in heaven" (Matt. 6:10). I often find myself clinging to that thought. God's kingdom in heaven is perfect, and I pray that His heavenly perfection will be ours on earth, and I long for that time. But then I have to roll up my sleeves and go visit somebody's grandma in the hospital or counsel with a couple contemplating divorce.

I once pastored a church in a tough neighborhood. One day a deputy sheriff came knocking on my door. When I opened it, he said, "We've got to take a seat from your church bus to the police station."

It was the last thing I expected to hear. "OK," I agreed, "but what for?"

"A girl just got raped on it."

In the church parking lot. Thirty yards from my front door. That's not the kingdom, but that's where churches are—and where they need to be.

Here I was wondering whether it was time for God to get me out of that place and put me in a nice suburban church with a better salary and a new car and a country club membership. But I was where God wanted me, doing just what God wanted me to do.

The kingdom church, the perfect church, is only in heaven. But every church exists to work toward and focus on kingdom perfection. Every church should be a kingdom-focused church. And every successful church is exactly that.

If you're in a kingdom-focused church, you're in a church that has a shape and dimension that God will decide. Once you realize what that means, then instead of running around after every program and how-to seminar that comes along, or trying to copy what works at Big Church, U.S.A., just because it works there, all of a sudden you can focus on the road ahead. One direction is obviously better than another because you know where you're going. Instead of a whiteout, you see the road signs clearly.

When you have a kingdom-focused church, the goal becomes more important than the mechanics. You stop looking frantically for the silver-bullet Sunday School curriculum and look at the ultimate destination for you and your fellowship of believers.

A church's kingdom focus has to come from outside the congregation—never from the inside. The focus of every successful church comes from the God of the universe, from heaven, His presence, and His reign. It is a kingdom focus because it comes from, rests in, and is empowered by the King.

The kingdom-focused church is one that has found its full meaning in the heart of God and in His actions toward all of us here on earth. It is broader than our understanding but not our experience. It is as majestic as the sky on a clear winter's night but as ordinary as a Sunday worship service. A kingdom-focused church reaches heights it cannot reach by itself and bends down to rescue persons from the depths of the sin it denounces. It is a community of ordinary saints used by God to accomplish extraordinary things. It is His perfect combination of heaven on earth.

The kingdom-focused church is constantly changing in every way except its nature and function. Every time someone joins the church or leaves it, it becomes a different place. It has bifocal vision, looking both up to heaven and down toward earth. It is filled with saints who look up toward the Lord with reverence and across the aisle at their fellow human beings with understanding.

Unlike other books you may have read about the life and function of the church (and I'm sure you and I have read many of the same ones), this book will drive straight to the heart of what every believer must understand about the nature and function of the church. My biggest challenge to conventional thinking about building a healthy church is this: you will never find the full meaning of your church or the pathway to a healthy, successful church in methods, conferences, and overhead transparencies. You will only find the full understanding of your church's life and mission in the heart of God and His will for you.

I love new ideas, especially new ideas that work, but I've been frustrated many times as a pastor and church leader with new ideas that didn't work when I tried them in my church.

If your seminar/conference/workbook experience is anything like mine, you've probably jumped on ideas from a variety of programs only to be disappointed when they didn't work for your congregation. As a matter of fact, I've winced many a time as a conference concluded or I finished the latest book on church growth and health, and I was admonished:

"Now, don't try this when you get back home!"

In other words, I can see why you might be skeptical at this point, with a tiny little voice inside warning that this book is going to be like all the rest.

But this book is different. This message is different. The message is that the answers you're looking for are not found, nor will they ever be, in someone else's successes, ideas, methods, or models. Your answer is in knowing the biblical model of a church and understanding how to conform your church—regardless of size, location, resources, history, or any other variable—to that biblical pattern. It is understanding where you are, which direction you need to head, and how to fix things when they break down along the way.

Let's face it, many churches all over the world are broken right now. People come into them and leave again without ever understanding what a local church is or how it's supposed to work according to God's kingdom plan. Methods and programs are useless without a fundamental biblical understanding of a church.

If you've labored in the vineyard long enough to become discouraged, working hard at things that don't work, I hope you'll give yourself the time to read this book carefully and prayerfully. I hope to share some things you may have heard about but never really thought about before. I hope you'll connect with some helpful ideas too, possibly things far outside the box of familiar ideas about church growth.

So read on until you get to the end, then go back and read it again. Read it by chapters, or part of a chapter at a time, until you've absorbed and fully understood everything here. I promise that you will be encouraged as you read and that as you go through the book you will become more sure of what you need to do to build a kingdom-focused church.

Above all, I encourage you to let God use what you learn from this book to change forever the way you experience church.

If your church isn't all it could be, becoming a kingdom-focused church will give you everything you need to achieve your full potential. Any other option will lead you to a smorgasbord of programs that, as often as not, do more harm than good by distracting you from the focus, nature, and mission of the church God has in mind for you.

I hope you'll read on to learn why a kingdom focus will work when everything else fails.

Chapter 2

THE CHURCH THAT WORKS

H EALTHY SKEPTICISM IS A GOOD THING whether you're looking for new ways to build a church or the secret to a better golf swing. One study I've seen claims that 87 percent of all institutional reorganization programs fail completely within the first two years.

Whether it's a big corporation, a nonprofit group, a church, or something else, the story is too often the same. The leadership of the organization gets hold of a new operational model or program that promises to eradicate all the waste, frustration, and inefficiency in the way they've operated in the past.

And so they go to retreats and seminars. They sit in on discussion groups and luncheon meetings. They read the workbook. They get the T-shirt. And once in a while they find answers that work. But most of the time they don't. There might be some fresh enthusiasm for a while, a new team spirit. Unfortunately, though, those good feelings usually melt away before long, leaving a thin residue of hope mixed with all-too-familiar feelings of frustration and defeat.

The big problem with the 87 percent of programs that fail is that they focus on mechanics and procedures instead of on results. You may be riding a different horse, but you find you're on the same old merry-go-round. Success comes when we have a clear vision of what

God wants from us. We set goals and manage everything we do to achieve maximum results. What this book presents *will* succeed because it deals with direction and focus instead of implementation. Its purpose is to draw a big "You Are Here!" sign, not a road map.

This book explains how to set your sights on becoming a kingdom-focused church. The method you need to use to get there depends on your individual congregation and what God wants to do through you. Don't waste your time trying to apply generic solutions or focusing on programs tailored for other believers in different kinds of communities. Pour your energy into a kingdom focus.

The kingdom-focused church is a church that works. It works the same way for city churches, country churches, big churches, small churches, traditional churches, contemporary churches, and every other kind because the kingdom-focused church has a shape that God alone will decide.

That should be good news for pastors and church leaders who have struggled and strained to "find a vision" for their church and felt defeated by their inability to do so. There are so many good pastors—like Mike, our example in the last chapter—who are at the end of their rope. "What are we going to do next?" they ask. "We're stuck! Nothing's working!" They think they've failed, and they beat themselves over the head with it. Or they suffer in silence, too ashamed to face what they see as a betrayal of their calling.

But when you have a kingdom-focused church, the pressure's off. You allow yourself and your ministry to be used as an instrument of God's will. You come alongside Him where He is at work and, lo and behold, you discover that the solution you've been wracking your brain for isn't programmatic or mechanical; it's spiritual. Then you realize that, hey, you're not really so terrible a pastor. God can truly use you for His work. You're not nearly the big zero you thought you were.

Chapter 16 of Ezekiel graphically describes a newborn baby that has been abandoned by its mother and "thrown out into the open field" (Ezek. 16:5b). Then God comes along and takes up the baby, washes it off, wraps it in white linen, and makes it His own. "I gave you my solemn oath and entered into a covenant with you, declares the Sovereign LORD, and you became mine" (Ezek. 16:8). God does the same thing with your church. You're a helpless mess without a kingdom focus. But once you have that focus, you have the direction and understanding you need for your church to take its rightful place in the kingdom.

Once a kingdom focus becomes your goal, worldly trappings and limitations become a lot less important. It's like when the apostle Paul wrote to Timothy, sort of fussing with him for being ashamed that Paul was in jail and suffering. He admonished Timothy to fulfill his ministry, keep going, and not give up. Timothy was discouraged and was using Paul's imprisonment as an excuse to throw in the towel.

With a kingdom-focused church, you can see that you don't have to give up in the face of difficulties. Paul encouraged Timothy not to quit but to fulfill his ministry—preach the word whether it is convenient or not to do the work of an evangelist (2 Tim. 4:1–8). There have been times in my pastoral ministry when, like Timothy, I wanted to give up. Like him, I felt hemmed in by all the worldly hassles that kept me from achieving what I wanted to do. Paul's advice was to look up from the methods and look ahead to the big picture: the kingdom focus that is the right and true goal of every church. Your kingdom call may be the only thing that keeps you where God has sent you.

Jesus underscores this goal in John 5:19–20 when He says, "I assure you: The Son is not able to do anything on His own, but only what He sees the Father doing. For whatever the Father does, these things the Son also does in the same way. For the Father loves the Son and shows Him everything He is doing, and He will show

Him greater works than these so that you will be amazed." God will show you and your church what to do.

In no more than twenty-five words, what exactly is a *kingdom-focused church?* It is a church that *exists to transform unbelievers into Christlike believers and to mature these believers into kingdom multipliers of the message of Christ.*

God saves the unsaved through the ministry of a kingdom-focused church, then inspires and equips the new believers so that others can be saved. One Christian delivers the good news to a number of people, who each witness to several more; each of those then witnesses to another group of the unsaved, and the message multiplies. A kingdom-focused church makes disciples, matures them through spiritual transformation, and multiplies them as kingdom agents throughout the world. Such a church has a passion to see every person complete in Christ.

In a kingdom-focused church, the emphasis is on the result and how to meet your people where they are spiritually, not on mechanical models, processes, or programs. It makes no effort to overlay someone else's solution on your need.

Emphasizing the process instead of the kingdom focus sends a lot of promising pastors to a dead end, especially if that process puts all the responsibility and pressure on the pastor alone. As we'll discuss in detail later on, the pastor isn't the church—the people are.

Even if Mike stops looking for the perfect church, he will not yet be out of the woods. He doesn't realize it—neither sees nor understands—but God is in control right now. Mike has had the benefit of the best theological training available. He has successfully made it through the struggles of starting in ministry. But what he now faces is beyond his experience and training.

Imagine that Mike is not a pastor but a race-car driver. He has been to a special Formula One Racing Institute and has passed with flying colors. He knows how to drive at staggering speeds and how to handle himself and a very expensive machine on any track. One day the phone rings, and he is thrilled when offered a contract to drive a car in the Indianapolis 500! He goes to the track. After the time trials he is placed in the starting lineup. Race day comes, the green flag drops, and he is off with the other racers. Twenty laps into the race something in the car is not right, and he pulls into the pit area. No one is there, so he drives behind the wall into the garage area, but no one is there.

He climbs out of the car and looks around. Every part, every tool, and every instrument he needs to repair his car is in the garage. The only problem is that he knows nothing about how his car really works. He can drive a functioning car; he just cannot fix one that is broken. Since he doesn't understand how it works, he might determine to change a seat or add a wheel. He might take a hammer and pound the fenders. He might change the wiper blades. But in the end he will not be able to get the car running again. Until he understands the engineering and mechanics of internal combustion engines, superchargers, rack and pinion steering, wind resistance, and a host of other technical details, his failure is certain.

The reality many pastors face isn't all that different. They're given the best training in Greek, Hebrew, homiletics, apologetics, philosophy, psychology, and the Bible. They are equipped with the skills required to run an already-efficient congregation. Most preachers can preach, greet people, and visit hospitals. Give them a well-oiled church, and they do well. Preaching, leading, and relating to people come naturally to them. But give them one that is broken or dysfunctional, and things don't go so well. An already efficient congregation is not what they're likely to find. What more often happens when they arrive at their first assignment is that they find a torn-up and broken church.

The trouble, however, is that they do not understand the nature of the church, its kingdom purpose, and how to fix what is broken. Their training has not prepared them to fix anything. So they attempt to correct the problems they face by changing methods, trying innovative techniques, preaching with more conviction, and leading with passion.

It's really unfair to do this to good young pastors, but it happens all the time.

I offer this illustration not as a criticism of seminaries. I am a product of one of the world's largest and best seminaries. What the men and women taught me there, I treasure and continue to benefit from greatly. We need a kingdom focus, and we need to learn *with* our seminaries, not just *from* them. It might surprise you, but, if anything, I think we need more training. No pastor or staff member is going to be hurt going deeper into studies in Greek, Hebrew, Old and New Testaments, and the classical and practical studies seminaries provide. What I would add is this: more understanding of a local church, what it is and how it works.

Another story that comes to mind is what happened to me one summer when I was sixteen. My responsibilities as the family lawn boy increased considerably when my father brought a new lawn mower home one day. Actually, it was only new in the sense that it had not been in our garage before. In fact, it was a piece of junk ready for any scrap heap that would take it. I remember looking at it with some doubt and suspicion, but my apprehension was easily dismissed by my father when he said, "Don't worry about how it looks. You can have it running like new in no time."

Like most sixteen-year-old boys, I did not often catch everything my father said. I mean, who can process a father's wisdom when there are important things to think about like dating, driving, sports, and summer fun. But that day he had all of my attention with the word, "*You* can have it running in no time." I have never been the sharpest among the many, but I know the meaning of *you*. That meant me, Gene Mims, son of V. O. and Margery Mims: sixteen, bold, and clueless.

To add to this pressure was the fact that my father could design, build, repair, and figure out *anything*. At that point in my life, I could do none of the above; and, knowing his demanding ways, I knew I was in trouble.

As we stood there looking at this relic, he seemed to sense what I was thinking and assured me with these deceptively simple instructions: "Just break everything down and remember what fits with what." This he followed with talk about new rings for the pistons, cleaning the needle valve, and adjusting the spark plug gap, after which I would need to sharpen the blade, minding the shear pins when I put it back on. And then of course there was the muffler.

By the time he finished his explanation, I was sweating more than normal for a summer day. My mouth was dry, and my mind clouded with a swirl of conflicting emotions running somewhere between panic and the despair only impending failure can bring.

He left and I went to work, reasoning that if others could do small-engine repair then so could I. After all, I had tools, a lawn mower, an assignment, and all afternoon. I took each piece of that lawn mower apart. In fact, it was easier than I thought it would be. Piece after piece separated under my deft touch until I had parts strewn across our garage floor. I washed everything in gasoline per instructions. Then I took the old rings off the pistons, and that's where the trouble began. I couldn't get the new ones on, so I turned my attention to the carburetor and my new friend, the needle valve. What was easy to remove was suddenly impossible to reattach. Did I mention the butterfly and linkage?

What I had disassembled I could not reassemble. I didn't understand how lawn mowers worked, how they were made, how they broke, or how to repair what was damaged.

You know what's funny about my lawn mower experience? I had basically the same feeling in my first church. I went in with great hopes and expectations, but then someone died, and I had to try to comfort the family. The church nearly split over painting the sanctuary. (I am not making this up!) Then someone told me about conducting Vacation Bible School six weeks after we had our annual revival. Soon after I arrived, a woman got angry with me for something I have never understood to this day, and our treasurer gave me a careful explanation of some financial "pressures" he thought we might be having. Those pressures included the lack of enough money to pay the electric bill, the water bill, and my salary.

I felt like I did that hot summer day when I could see lawn mower parts scattered all over my garage. My church issues were scattered like that, and I did not know what to do. I didn't even know how things worked or why.

There was no kingdom in my focus because, in spite of my seminary training, I didn't know any better. Now, more than thirty years later, I've done enough pastoring and talked with enough pastors that I can sit down with somebody who's telling me about his church and know in about five minutes whether he's heading for heartache. More often than not, God's trying to order his life into cycles, but he's living it in circles instead.

Programs depend on people and resources, while a kingdom focus does not. A kingdom focus is utterly dependent on God. People sitting out there in the pews don't give their lives to Christ because they like up-tempo music or great Sunday School lessons—though those things might appeal to them on the surface. They commit their lives to Jesus because they see the need in their lives and because they recognize that Jesus can satisfy in a way nothing else can. And so to the extent your music and Sunday School classes direct the people in your church toward the kingdom, they're the right thing to do.

When conditions change or people come and go in the church, programs will eventually become obsolete or ineffective. Churches change over time because change is inevitable. But with a kingdom focus you don't have to abandon the future of your church to the forces of random change. You might have to change your tactics, but your objective is timeless.

Churchgoers—members, visitors, and seekers alike—aren't overly concerned about the preacher's education or finer points of doctrine. They're worried about themselves, their jobs, their families; they come to church with real needs. What's lacking too often is a promise from the church concerning the path to transformation into Christlikeness. If we'll spend time with them and focus on the right objective, we'll know how to make and realize that promise.

Over the past four years, I have spent some time surfing the Internet. During those years I have researched topics that relate to the nature and function of a church. I have read many articles, sermons, and statements on the subject. I have joined chat rooms and enjoyed dialogue with professionals as well as laymen as we discussed various topics surrounding the nature and functions of a church.

More importantly, I have spent many hours in private conversation with pastors of all kinds of churches. I am fortunate to be in a position that allows me access to people from around the world who know about church life and health. I have enjoyed many great hours of dialogue and discussion about church and what it means today.

These experiences in reading, talking, listening, and learning have given me some understanding of what many persons are feeling about the church today. I hasten to say that while my comments are not based on scientific models, they are solid as qualitative models often are. My observations are just that, opinions and feelings based on many conversations and thirty years' experience.

Most of what is said about church tends to be seasonal and transitory. In less than ten years we have changed our vocabulary on church issues several times. There is no single way to describe the nature and functions of a church. It remains a spiritual mystery, and those like me who tend to comment on church and its role today have to be careful. It is easy to be wrong, easier to be misunderstood, and easiest to be outdated quickly.

Most predictions about church made by researchers, pastors, and social commentators are wrong. They are not necessarily wrong in part but wrong in the whole. It is simply impossible to speak definitively about "the church." There are too many congregations to do that accurately. Each local church has its own style, culture, shape, priorities, and expectations.

I truly believe that:

Methods are many, principles are few;

Methods may change, principles never do.

I can no longer keep up with the many methods of organizing and running a church, nor can I always keep pace with the changes in vocabulary that interpret the methods. I have come to realize that they are too many and too dynamic to worry about for long.

I often find myself listening to pastors who explain why and how the methods they are using work best for them. As they extol what they are doing, I find myself thinking how those very things would tear most other churches completely to pieces. It is amazing how alike and yet how different local churches are from one another. It is a paradox we should never forget.

I have enjoyed reading many current writers on church issues. Every one of them speaks with passion for the people of God and for those who lead our churches. The list of their books has no end, and the number of observations, exhortations, suggestions, and resources are far too numerous to track. I hesitate somewhat to throw my thoughts out there with so many others, but I have chosen to for several reasons.

These reasons form the value proposition for this book. If you read this book, I want to make you several promises.

First, I want you to know that what I'm sharing works. I have seen the value and the power of a kingdom focus for over thirty years. What I am writing down, I have experienced firsthand in many different situations and churches. (I used to wonder why the Lord allowed me to lead such different congregations, but now I think I know!)

I have pastored in rural America right in the middle of a cotton field. I have pastored in a transitional community. I have led a church in a depressed and sometimes violent community and one in a pristine suburb. I have pastored churches in county seat towns, small cities, large cities, near military bases, and in developing suburban areas. Small, large, mega, declining, growing—you name it, and it has been mine to lead as pastor, staff member, or interim pastor.

Second, these ideas are not only based on my experience as a leader but on my experience as an expositor of Scripture. In short, they are biblical. I offer no apology for their biblical basis because I must confess that I have no use for church principles that are not biblically based. In fact, I am a ready critic of any resource not grounded in Scripture. It pains me to read many current resources on leadership, worship, church growth, and discipleship that are no more than spiritual parroting of popular secular ideas.

Third, within the pages of this book, you will find a pathway to a kingdom focus that underlies what any and every church must fulfill in order to see every person complete in Christ. Too many things in our churches today simply do not link together. They do not fit, and they will not cause churches to fulfill the Great Commission. I am not opposed to any ministry, program, emphasis, or anything else that helps us to reach lost people for Christ and leads them through maturity to a multiplying ministry. But programs, preaching, worship services, and buildings will never do this. There is a lesson inherent in Scripture for a church to accomplish the Great Commission. In this book you not only will discover what this lesson is, but you also will learn how to implement it into your own unique ministry and church.

Fourth, this entire book is focused on and based on the kingdom of God. Church renewal in our world is largely dependent on our understanding of the kingdom of God and the church's relationship to it. Until we do, I can assure you that we will continue to work hard at the things that ultimately do not work. The fundamental reality in our world today is the kingdom of God, but unfortunately many Christian leaders have no clue of its worth and importance.

Fifth, I can promise you that if you stay with me until the end of this book, your understanding of what to do next in your church will be matched only by your passion to know and serve the living God. God is at work in this world, and He is inviting us to join Him. I want to show you how to join practical action to that wonderful truth. It is one thing to know God is at work. It is another actually to join Him with the assurance that you are doing exactly what He wants you and your church to do.

Finally, I promise you that once you understand the nature of a church in relationship to the kingdom of God and the world we now live in, God will lead you to fix whatever is wrong with your church. Yes, you read right. I promise that once you understand what this book has to say, you will have all you need to fix *everything* that's wrong with your church, no matter what it is. Every church is special to the Lord, and every pastor and every church leader is called to serve

His churches. You can do it well, but it takes understanding of what you have to do, knowledge of the nature of a local church, faith in God and His Word. And, finally, it takes time. It takes time to get whatever is broken fixed.

Please enjoy what you read. Think about it. Pray about it. Know in your heart that He who called you to this great work cannot fail you, and you have no reason ever to fail Him. God is working to redeem His creatures from their sin and separation from Him. His kingdom is sure, it's here now, and we are called to spread its gospel and truth across the earth. I join you in seeking the Lord and His ways in this generation.

Chapter 3

THE—
AN ARTICLE OF FAITH

IT IS NOT UNUSUAL OR UNLIKELY that Mike would dream about another church. Most of us are dreamers by nature. We are visionaries, and we like to think about what can be or what might be. If we didn't, we could never lead anyone to do anything better or differently. But the danger for a visionary is subtle. Dreams can replace reality if we are not careful. And whatever a church is, it is *real!* Mike will make a serious mistake if he continues to dream about another church in another place. His calling is to the Lord, and it is the Father's prerogative to send him wherever He chooses.

Mike is a fine pastor, and he will eventually get through this phase in his life and ministry if he can remember a few fundamental things.

A good start is to remember that God calls us to Himself and sends us to serve one of His churches. It is a mistake to believe that a church calls a pastor. His calling is always from the Lord to Himself—to a dynamic relationship of love, fellowship, and service. It is also God who sends us to the places He wants us to serve Him and His people. If the Lord is responsible for my place of service, then I can stay in and through the tough times. I can endure hardship as a minister. I can love the Lord and love the people I reach for Christ and the believers

I serve. I can exhibit faithful endurance as the Lord works through me and through His people to accomplish His purposes.

Pastor Mike will have to set aside his daydreams and focus on the church he currently pastors. The issue is neither how long nor how much. His focus is not on how many or how few he reaches. His concern is three-dimensional. First, he must walk with the Lord in a living faith. To be a Christian leader you have to learn how to follow. My colleague John Kramp has done a great job of explaining this idea in his book *Getting Ahead by Staying Behind.* He writes:

> Jesus' mission on earth was a search-and-rescue operation with an unusual twist—in this case, the lost were in an enviable position. For Jesus, the term *lost* was not derogatory. Being lost implied there was some place you were supposed to be and someone who cared that you were not there. . . . In effect, God said, "You're supposed to be in a relationship with Me, but you're separated from Me. That means you are lost. And because you are lost, I will pay the ultimate price to rescue you. . . ."
>
> If God's only goal was to rescue us, He could have zapped us straight to heaven once we became Christians so we could bypass the inevitable struggles of earth. But He didn't. He left us here—not forever, but for now. Obviously, something we do from the time we "get found" to the time we join Him in eternity is important. We "get found" so that we can follow. The process of following Jesus on earth changes us. That's why Jesus repeatedly gave a simple invitation during His earthly ministry: "Follow Me." That's why Jesus extends the same invitation to us today. . . .
>
> After His crucifixion and resurrection, Jesus met again with His disciples. All had failed Him,

especially Peter, who had denied Him three times.
But Jesus offered forgiveness and hope and extended
a new call to discipleship by evoking the same lan-
guage He had used to extend the initial call to disci-
pleship years before: "Then [Jesus] said to him,
'Follow me!' Peter turned and saw that the disciple
whom Jesus loved was following them. . . . When
Peter saw him he asked, 'Lord, what about him?'
Jesus answered, 'If I want him to remain alive until
I return, what is that to you? You must follow me'"
(John 21:19–22, NIV).[1]

After we learn to follow Christ, then we can learn to lead others
to Him.

Second, he must determine what the Lord wants done and what
God is currently doing in the life of His people and community.
Third, he must concentrate on building up his people so they can get
on God's agenda—fulfilling the Great Commission.

Book titles fascinate me. I often pick up an unfamiliar book
because of the title but then discover that the title doesn't match the
content of the book. *The Kingdom-Focused Church* is an exception.
Each word has been chosen with a great deal of thought, discussion,
and prayer: *The, Kingdom, Focused, Church*. I chose each word so that
the title outside accurately describes the contents inside.

I didn't necessarily look for a title with a good marketing hook
or something that would play to your personal interest (though
I hope it does). This is a book about the focus of a church and how
the correct focus ultimately determines every church's health and
effectiveness.

The first word in the title is one of the most common, most
innocuous words in the English language. It's so common and
generic, in fact, that it's perfectly reasonable to think, "Hey, let's blow

right past that little fella and get on to the serious stuff." But in our context, this little article has something important to say.

The denotes a *particular* congregation of the church universal, with its own unique challenges and opportunities: *The* church God has put you in right now. If you want a healthy church, a growing church, an exciting church, then all you have to do is look around at what you have and get busy.

The church is the church where you pastor, lead, serve, belong, or attend. God has given you a stewardship position in this particular church. He hasn't put you in a church somewhere else, and He hasn't given another church your unique gifts, potential, and vision. If you're a pastor, that means for this time and place, God thinks the best pastor in the world for your church is *you.*

For the present, you're not responsible for another church in the entire world. Think about it for a minute. Aren't you delighted and relieved that the Lord hasn't given you responsibility for every church in your city? Isn't it a good thing that all the churches in your town are not dependent on your stewardship? Aren't you relieved to know all those churches you drove by on your vacation last year aren't sitting around waiting for you to tell them what to do?

As part of a particular church, you shouldn't be distracted by other churches that seem to have fewer problems than yours. Your whole heart should be poured into the church where you are, not some nonexistent, imaginary, perfect church in Coulda-Shoulda-Wouldaville. No halfhearted commitment, no complaining. Where you are now is where God placed you and where you belong.

That doesn't mean that you should realistically expect to serve in the same church all your life. In God's good time people do move from one congregation to another for all sorts of reasons. But a lot of people I've known over the years have been too impatient to let God work things out as He saw best.

One result of this impatience is that there's an unhealthy and counterproductive level of turnover in churches. It takes a long time to pastor a church and get to the point where you can touch the spiritual core of your people. I'd say it takes seven to ten years on average to develop that level of mutual trust. But so many pastors leave one congregation for another with the job unfinished! They haven't had time to fulfill God's vision for them in that place. In fact, the pattern of leaving too soon too often means you will *never* pastor a church. If it really takes seven to ten years to become the pastor of a church and we move every four or five years, *then we never really pastor a church!*

Sometimes it's the congregation's fault. Influential members become dissatisfied and insist that the pastor be booted. Sometimes it's the fault of the denominational hierarchy. The ruling leadership reassigns a pastor before his work is really complete. Sometimes it's the pastor's doing. He's looking for the next career move and is overeager to polish his résumé.

The image of a company president and a board of directors comes to mind. "Jones, you've got eighteen months to meet these performance criteria or we're going to show you the door and give the job to the next guy on the list." It's so important to remember, as we'll explore in detail later, that a church isn't a business, and a successful church can't be operated like one. A church—your church—is a ministry before it's anything else. A church has some surface similarities with a corporate organization; but its goals, timetables, and vision are different. To put corporate pressures on a pastor is sinful and devastating.

So the bottom line is that you and your church belong together. Now before the grumbling gets too loud, let me remind you of the process you went through before you came to serve the church where you are today. If you're a pastor, you thought long and hard about the call. You prayed about it, talked with your family about it, probably called up a mentor or trusted friend and asked his opinion. If you're a church leader, my guess is that you looked at a lot of candidates, prayed, and sought the wisdom of a lot of members of the congregation before you selected (or called or approved or requested, depending on your denomination) the pastor you have now.

Whichever side of the fence you were on, you probably remember something about "the will of God" or "the Lord's leading" as the decision was being made. The fit seemed so right somehow. The prospective pastor and the search committee had such deep, fulfilling conversations leading up to the decision and during the period of transition. From those conversations and all those good feelings, everybody shared a deep conviction that this congregation and this pastor would be a perfect match.

As pastors, remember that when you came to the church you're presently serving—*the* church—expectations were high both for you and for the people. Even though you knew from the start that the church wasn't exactly perfect, you felt confident you could come in and make a difference. Your leadership ability and desire matched their needs, and you were willing to work as hard as necessary to be successful.

What happened? Where did the dream go? What about God's calling you and sending you there? Trouble, heartache, and disappointment do not set aside the call of God.

At some point that boundless enthusiasm and the sense that anything was possible seeped slowly away, replaced by a sobering dose of reality. How did you lose your passion for the job? Did someone hurt you or your family? Did you discover that some of your people aren't as faithful or supportive today as they were when you came? Were there times when you felt your people trusted you and you let them down? Did you make what you thought was a fatal mistake from a career-advancement perspective?

These are only a few of the questions that help identify some of the problems and disappointments you face as a pastor leading your church. But here's an important fact to keep in mind: getting answers to your questions and understanding your disappointments does not release you from the task of pastoring people and leading them to do what God wants done in our communities.

No matter how tired, hurt, frustrated, or burned out you are at this moment, you have a church to lead, a church where God has placed you because right now you're the best person for the job. Your focus must begin with *the* church you have.

You have a sacred responsibility and calling over one church and one church only right now, and your mandate is to make it *the* kingdom-focused church. No matter how universal, global, denominational, or invisible you understand the church to be, your focus must begin with *the* church that is looking to you for leadership.

But having put all this responsibility on pastors and ministers, we can't ignore the other side of the equation. No pastor can lead a church that refuses to be led. Congregations have to be willing to embrace the mandate of the Great Commission to carry the gospel of Jesus far and wide. Every kingdom-focused church exists to lead unbelievers to become believers and believers into mature multipliers of the message of Christ. The people of your church have to be willing to minister. This means that in the same way a pastor has to get past all the distractions of the moment and lead, his congregation has to put church politics and divisiveness behind them and follow.

I know from firsthand experience that far too many church members live in isolated, self-perpetuating clusters. They're like frogs on lily pads floating around in a pond that bump into one another once in a while. Except for bumping into one another for an hour on Sunday morning, these clusters have nothing to do with one another. They may, in fact, be working in opposite directions for mutually exclusive purposes. (Though I've seen this plenty of times, I know it's never happened in your church!)

When a congregation gets too muddled up in its own agenda, it's the pastor's responsibility to bring the fact to their attention. This isn't always the most popular thing for a preacher to do, but it is always the right thing.

If leaders or members of a congregation are looking for the church that ought to be, they're in big trouble because they can never attend a church that "ought to be." They can only attend *the* church where they are now. Wherever they "ought to be," they're going to have to "ought to be" some other time.

There is no perfect church. But if you insist on continuing the quest for one, there are two things you can do that will truly help *the* church you're in. Either stop looking, or look somewhere else. Now this is not an overly popular suggestion, but I've got to speak the truth in love here. The best thing people who feel that way can do for the church is to find *the* church where God wants them to serve.

You may have a burning desire to say to people like that, "You ought to quit whining and go back to the Scriptures and see how your church measures up and how it got that way." First Downtown Church is just what it is. It can be better and it can be worse, but today it's what it is. It's full of frogs on their little lily pads bumping into one another once in a while. But that's not what a kingdom-focused church is, and no preacher can change that. That's got to be taken care of by the frogs themselves. If they can't fix it, how can they expect a pastor to fix it for them? All the preaching in the world won't help them.

Congregations have to realize that no preacher can lead them where they don't want to go. He can't lead them to minister if they refuse to minister. He can't lead them to love if they're intent on being mean. They can change pastors every year for the next fifty years, and nothing will change until they're willing to change.

I often say to pastor search committees, I don't think you're going to call somebody who can swoop in and fix your mess. He's coming to equip you to minister. Trying to do anything else is like trying to put something together when you don't understand the instructions. (Reassembling the many parts of a lawn mower comes to mind.)

One year I got my dad a fancy outdoor barbecue grill for Father's Day and decided to put it together for him in secret the night before. You know the story: "Some assembly required." I got off to a promising start, but after a while I found out to my dismay that Sub-Assembly A didn't even come close to lining up with Bottom Plate B. The harder I worked, the worse the situation got.

About the time I'd decided to give up and let my dad put it together himself, my cousin came over. He took a look at the instructions and had the whole grill together in fifteen minutes. With the right kind of help, following those instructions was simple; without it I was lost. If your new pastor tries to assemble a new church without the right kind of help, he's doomed to failure.

In the same way that every church has its own characteristics, needs, and opportunities, every church has its own future. What's your view about the future of your church? I've been in churches where people talked all the time about *potential*: "This church has all kinds of potential."

When anybody starts to talk to me about potential, I know things are really bad. Whatever potential you have is based on what you are today. That's the only potential you have. If your church is a dud now, it will still be a dud a year from now unless you take specific action to make it something else.

Is it your heartbeat to see everybody in your church complete in Jesus Christ? That means that they become everything God has created them to become. These are real live people who are able to be complete in Christ as they go through all the muddy waters of marriage, as they face uncertainties of family, as they gain and lose jobs, and as they are depressed and need help. Do you have a passion for the people there in *the* church where God has placed you? To see every person become the man, the woman, the little boy, the little girl, the young person that God wants them to be?

I'm going to confess something. I've always had a passion to see people saved. This has always been a major part of my life and ministry. But sometimes I've been more passionate about seeing people come to First Baptist Church than to the kingdom. Or more passionate to see them be Baptists than Christians.

That is so wrong. It is possible to take pride in your church and forget that you are a part of the kingdom. You can make your church an infirmary in a sin-sick world. But the goal of this church is not to be the infirmary. I'm glad the army has field hospitals where we can take our wounded and take care of them. Maybe you have been wounded and somebody took care of you in a field hospital. Still, the point of the army is not to have field hospitals but to have soldiers engaged in battle. The point of a church is not only to be a Christian critical care center but a spiritual army teeming with well-trained soldiers of the cross doing battle in the world.

Your success as an individual church isn't going to be determined by the plans you have. It's going to be according to the decisions you make and what you do to act upon those decisions. Do you wait around and hope your job will be better? Do you wait and hope your dinner will get cooked or your garage will get painted? Of course not. You decide what color to paint it, get the equipment you need, and get to work. You've got to look at your church the same way.

The reminders that every church has its own place, its own life, and its own future—and that, for better or worse, every church changes—are all around us. Each day I make a thirty-minute commute from my home to my office in Nashville, Tennessee. I listen to the radio to get the latest traffic and weather information and think about the day ahead. At my exit from Interstate 40, my eyes often drift over toward an adult bookstore. It is trimmed in a garish shade of purple and advertises the latest in X-rated books, tapes, and videos. There aren't many cars there when I go by at 6:30 A.M., but sometimes a few are parked in the lot.

When I see that bookstore, my heart always sinks a bit. It's not because of what the store is and sells. I hate pornography and how it attracts people into its madness. I hate how pornography cheapens all of us and destroys what God has made to be good and enjoyable. But that's not what really gets me about this particular bookstore. In fact, it's really not what the building is now and what it is used for. It is what it used to be.

The lines of the building are unmistakable in its setting against downtown Nashville. They are as unique as the state capitol building at the top of the hill and as straightforward as the historic Union Station or the soaring hotels that punctuate the city skyline. You see, the adult bookstore used to be a church. That's right. Some time ago it was a church, no doubt filled with people seeking and serving God.

Over the years, though, things changed. I often wonder how and what things changed to make a thriving congregation move away and this particular bookstore to move in. Was it the Interstate that cut the church off from its community? Interstates are concrete rivers, often isolating people from communities, businesses, and churches. Maybe that's what happened. Or perhaps it was something else. Maybe the leadership changed and the people lost their vision. I don't make any judgments about why someone sold a church to a business. I just wonder why an adult bookstore can flourish in the same space where a church died.

Churches change with the passing of time. Some get stronger and some weaker, but all churches change. This process is inevitable but also manageable. You don't have to abandon *the* church you have right now to the forces of random change. No, you can begin today to make the kinds of change that will ensure a strong congregation no matter what happens to your community. You can see your church in light of the kingdom of God and equip your people to meet every challenge of their lives. You can be a presence in your community that will transcend all changes, threats, and adversities.

It's up to you and your church to do the will and the work of God in *the* church where you are now. It is a high calling to a high life of labor for the Lord. You can set your kingdom work against the background of your community and never have to give an inch to the creeping destruction of evil and the change it brings. You and your people today can determine not to give one more inch to the devil, to the world system that always stands against the Lord's will, or to the lusts of the men and women who live in your community.

Pour your heart into *the* church God has given you. I pray that you will joyfully bear the burdens and hardships of kingdom leadership there until your people are transformed into Christlikeness. And I pray that at the same time you're wrestling with the everyday needs of your church on earth, you can look up and look ahead for inspiration and assurance to the perfect glory of God's kingdom.

Stop right now and ask God to give you the courage to seek Him, to know His will and do it. Ask Him for the strength to lead your people and love them as He loves them. Ask Him to show you your church and community as He sees them. Humbly ask Him to show you what He desires your church to be in the future.

Thank the Lord for calling and choosing you. Surrender your life and work to His purpose. Take a stand today and lead your people in *the* church where you've been called.

And now let's see what an understanding of God's kingdom and His will can do to help make your church the best church it can be.

Chapter 4

KINGDOM—
REALITY CHECK

THE LOOK ON THE YOUNG WOMAN'S FACE told me she still had a question. I had just finished speaking to a group at her church about the kingdom of God, and several of us were standing around afterward visiting. She was not there, however, to enjoy the fellowship and conversation.

After hesitating for a minute, she came up to me and said, "Could I ask you something about what you said tonight?"

"Of course," I replied. "Let's grab a seat right here on the front row."

"I just don't understand," she began. "I've read the Bible for years, and I have never seen what you were talking about tonight. I've always understood that my life as a Christian is centered in my marriage, my family, and my church. But tonight you were talking about something I've absolutely never heard of before."

I encouraged her to try to remember any point in her life that she had been taught about the kingdom of God or read about it in Scripture.

She sat thinking for a few seconds then said, "I always thought of the kingdom of God as something that's coming at the end of the age when Christ comes back to earth. I never understood that what Jesus taught had any significance for me in the present."

As she talked, I thought back to the many times we make discoveries in our lives that have been right in front of us all the time but for some reason we couldn't see or find them. It's like each time I lose my keys, wallet, airline tickets, pens, or other personal items. They are always nearby, right where I left them, but for whatever reason I can't see them.

The kingdom of God is like that for most believers: it's there, but somehow they can't see it. Jesus was explicit in His teaching about the kingdom. In His first sermon in Galilee, His words centered on the kingdom of God, but it's easy to miss His meaning. He said, "The time is fulfilled, and the kingdom of God has come near. Repent and believe in the good news!" (Mark 1:15). Sandwiched in the middle of those two short sentences is the thrust of Jesus' message: the kingdom of God is here and now.

Now back to my conversation.

"Well," she went on, "I must admit I've read about the kingdom of God, but frankly, I'm confused. What is the kingdom that Jesus talks about? Where is it now? Am I in it, or am I going to get in it at some time in the future?"

She shifted in her seat and continued. "You see, when you talk about the kingdom of God, I'm not sure what you mean."

We talked a long time that night. I explained to her that in the Bible, the *kingdom* means the reign of God in the lives of His people, enabling them to serve Him wholeheartedly and to live the kind of life Jesus died to give us. In other words, the *kingdom* of God, in its simplest form, is the reign of Jesus Christ as Lord and King in our lives. It is His Holy Spirit working in us, through us, and around us in such a way that we actually live and do the will of God. Through the kingdom we can live the lives God created us to live—life at the maximum.

This is real Christianity! This is what the Lord wants each of us to have. This is the life that separates true Christians from people who do Christian things. Once you understand this, you will never again think as you once did about what a church is and why you go there. You will not live your life the same way, and you will know contentment that you have only dreamed of in the past.

The *kingdom* has nothing to do with obscure doctrine or difficult rules. It's about living the life that God intends for you to have. It is a life worth finding, a life worth living, and a life of genuine joy and excitement. Life in the kingdom of God is not a sheltered, careful life without risk, failure, achievement, or excitement. It's a life that's real in that everything we face is real. Life is filled with good and bad. We have joy alongside our sorrows and triumphs along with our defeats. Kingdom living is not an escape. It is an engagement. It is living at the highest human level even in the midst of the lowest human experience. It is full throttle, wide open, going straight ahead to an indescribable life.

The term *kingdom* is used in the Bible in several ways. Sometimes it refers to the universal reign of God over all creation. God is sovereign over all the universe, and in that sense everything is under His domain. Sometimes the kingdom is a direct reference to the nation of Israel. Israel was designed to be a theocracy (a nation ruled by God), and even when kings were anointed, everyone understood that God reigned over His people in the nation of Israel. A third use is the most often understood, and that is the coming earthly reign of Christ at His return. The fourth usage is the present rule of Christ in the lives of His people. And every successful church focuses on this use of *kingdom.*

The kingdom of God is the ultimate reality in the universe, and until we understand it and live under its truths, we cannot live our lives to their full potential. Right now, as you read this, the kingdom of God is present in our world and in every person in whom the Lord reigns as King. The *kingdom* is real, and it is yours.

Jesus made the kingdom of God the central focus of His teaching, preaching, ministry, and life. He described His fellowship of believers as "the church" only twice in the Gospels, but He referred to the kingdom nearly ninety times. The kingdom is an experience of God in daily life. Seeing the kingdom is seeing the world the way God sees it, like having on night-vision goggles.

Since your first days in Sunday School, you've been told to seek the kingdom of God, but you can't do that if you don't know what it is. It's like going on a snipe hunt—"you'll know it when you see it." But you're not sure what you're supposed to be looking for or what to do if you find it. A snipe hunt may be futile, but the *kingdom* is available and worth pursuing. It's real, and it's real life in Christ!

Many of us don't relate well to any concept of a king or a kingdom. When we think of a king, we imagine some romantic image of Camelot or perhaps a negative notion of a corrupt ruler. Monarchs and monarchies don't have a lot of appeal to Americans, and so when we talk about the kingdom of God, our thoughts can get muddled.

It reminds me of the old saying I heard when I was little, "That's as clear as mud!" It was my relatives' way of saying, "I heard the words, but I don't understand what you mean." To many Christians the kingdom of God is about as clear as mud. We are taught little about it, so as a result our understanding of and excitement about kingdom things is simply absent from our lives.

It's a lot easier in Great Britain. The monarchy there is a treasured and cherished institution. Even in the United States there is a high level of interest in the British royal family. But having an interest in and respect for a traditional monarchy still isn't the same as understanding what the kingdom of God truly means. To gain an appreciation for God's kingdom, we have to go back in time to the days when Jesus lived and ministered on earth.

First-century Jews better understood the concept of a kingdom because they were accustomed to seeing kings and queens in positions of authority. In fact, their history is filled with kings, queens, and rulers in Israel and Judah, as well as in the surrounding nations. The exploits of Saul, David, Solomon, and others were legendary in Israel. The lives and times of the kings were important enough that four books of the Old Testament are given to nothing but the history and fortunes of Israel and Judah under the leadership of these kings.

There was never any mistake in the minds of Jews wherever they were that Jehovah God was truly King of the nation and King of the nations. David, Israel's most beloved king, wrote and sang these words long ago:

> Your kingdom is an everlasting kingdom;
>
> Your rule is for all generations (Ps. 145:13).

Another psalmist wrote:

> The LORD is King forever (Ps. 10:16).

The prophet Isaiah wrote magnificent words to express the coming hope of Israel in the announcement of the coming Messiah. In expressing the wonder of proclaiming the good news of this coming, he wrote in Isaiah 52:7:

> How beautiful on the mountains
>
> are the feet of those who bring good news,
>
> who proclaim peace,
>
> who bring good tidings,
>
> who proclaim salvation,
>
> who say to Zion,
>
> "Your God reigns!" (NIV).

The allegiance of the Israelites to God was fundamental and required, but whether they acknowledged Him or not, the Lord was King over all things.

He still is.

The kingdom of God is the highest reach of our faith and lives. It is the arena where the person of the Lord is on full display. It is the place where truth meets us and makes perfect sense, the place where we walk by faith and not by sight only. It is what every believer hopes for and lives for each day, the place where the will of God is done without question. The kingdom is the place where the Lord is magnified and glorified.

The kingdom of God is where we long to be, free from sin, temptation, and the destruction of the world we see around us. The kingdom of God is the grand, full view of all we are in Christ the Lord. It is the full revelation of the great purposes of a sovereign God. His nature, His dominion, His rule, His subjects are here.

The kingdom is the place of His universal and cosmic purposes overcoming the sin and rebellion of His children. It is the place where creation, redemption, His people, His purposes, and His power all come together to make perfect sense to us as we experience His presence. We only begin to understand ourselves in light of the truth, wisdom, and the person of our sovereign, triune God! It is where heaven and earth meet in the person and reign of Christ.

The kingdom of God is the place where everything is always right, all the time. The kingdom of God is the beauty and glory of God where He is exalted and reigns. The kingdom is coming when Jesus Christ comes again to earth. When He comes, the kingdom that we experience in our hearts will be seen in a way that no one can imagine right now.

Can you grasp how crucial it is for you to understand fully the kingdom of God? If this clear understanding of the kingdom of God in today's world is absent:

- We will fail to see God at work around us.
- We will have little confidence in what Christ has done, is doing, and will do.
- We will try to do things for Him and never experience Him doing things through us.
- We will not pray effectively, go as commanded, give our lives, or endure the hardships of ministry as we must if we are to fulfill God's calling on our lives.

"Pastor Mike," a voice called from the hallway outside his office. "Hey man, it's me," called John. John pastors in the same city as Mike, and they are becoming best friends. "What's up, Mike?" he asked.

"Oh, nothing. I'm just sitting here wondering how potential gets transformed into reality around here," Mike replied.

"Well, I don't have all the answers," said John, "but I know that God has a perfect plan for us and our churches, even if we can't always see it. I think that we have to get in touch with His kingdom agenda and not lose sight of where we are ultimately going."

John is helping Mike to understand one of the primary tasks of leading a church. Every church must have a kingdom focus. In order to have a kingdom focus, a pastor must understand the true nature of the kingdom of God. Remember that the kingdom was the main focus of Jesus' earthly life, teaching, preaching, and ministry. He called us to that kingdom, and we are its citizens and leaders.

The kingdom of God is not a resource to use, a theory to explore, or an event to await. It is the fundamental reality in our world—an experience of God in daily life. Through it, we gain understanding of all that surrounds us. We see in it the victory we long for and the hope we have in Christ. It's not a dream, a notion, or an unrealistic longing. It is God's presence in our lives and in our world accomplishing His every purpose.

When I get tracking on the kingdom, even during my worst days, I feel as if I'm soaring up to something. When I get back to the church, I feel that I'm here to roll up my sleeves. Instead of trying to build "my" kingdom on five acres of land, I now see the *kingdom* for what it is.

The kingdom of God is where everything is perfect. The kingdom of God is where the Lord rules and reigns and the angels attend to Him. But we're down here on earth where life is real. Earth is where wars and rumors of wars and famines occur, a place where people's lives get messed up. Earth is where people get murdered and divorce happens and family members break apart. This is where disease inflicts people, and the church is in the middle of all that. We're not immune to any of it. So don't talk about the church as you think it ought to be—perfect. That's just living in a dream world. Earth is where life really happens.

Think of it as a sort of bifocal vision—the problems and hassles and daily troubles are here below, and the perfection of God's kingdom is in heaven.

What's our connection then to the kingdom? As believers we have these three primary relationships that come directly out of our salvation in Christ—our relationship with the kingdom, with the church universal, and with the church particular.

When God saved you by His grace in Christ, He put you into a living, dynamic, and eternal relationship with Him. You became His child through faith, and you remain His child forever. There will never be a time in your life from now on that you will not be related to Him. You will be free to worship Him for the rest of your time on earth, and you will worship Him in heaven forever.

Your salvation immediately brings you into other relationships as well. You are part of a family that began at creation and continues until we all reach heaven together. In the present you are in relationships with all true believers across the world. We are alike in our salvation through Christ even though we may not live near one another, have the same skin color or language, or have the same outlook on the world. At the same time we are part of a local body of believers—the church particular.

How awesome to be part of the same *kingdom* of Christ who reigns in the lives of His people! Right here. Right now.

Chapter 5

FOCUSED—
THE 20/20 VISION

I T's MONDAY AGAIN, and Mike is at his desk looking with despair at the events scheduled this week. He knows intuitively that he cannot get everything done. The pressure is building, and his frustration is rising. Never in his life did he think he would be whipped by something. His previous success in school, athletics, and life in general helped build his self-esteem and confidence. But pastoring is more difficult than he ever imagined. How can he get through the array of opportunities, demands, and details to get himself and the church moving?

Something has to happen. He is weary of doing things that don't work and of running in a circle of routine with no visible results. If you have ever tired of doing the things that don't work, read on. The journey is just beginning.

If I have made one discovery in the last ten years, it's that most churches do not have a kingdom *focus*. This means they don't have a Great Commission focus either. Without a Great Commission focus, the programs and ministries that are conducted every week don't fit together naturally and often seem to compete with one another. When things get stale or folks begin to stay away, the programs are changed and new ministries are added.

Does this sound familiar? You have added program after program, method upon method, but nothing really changed. Your people were not any more transformed, any more faithful or willing to serve, despite your best efforts. Do you ever feel like a marketing representative for a secular company as you push, promote, and promise great return on all those programs, events, and resources?

I've made another interesting discovery as well. When new programs, products, events, and methods are added, *nothing is ever taken away!* Even the smallest churches try to do too much, requiring more and more time and resources, yet delivering less and less. Do you ever get weary working hard at the things that don't work? I do, and I know you do. Don't you ever want to stop everything and just start over again?

Focus—it's easy enough to understand but difficult to do. I have promised you that we would discover some things that you can do to have a fulfilling ministry and a healthy church, but to do so, we have to at least acknowledge some of the problems. Problem 1 is almost invariably the lack of *focus.*

If you asked average church members why they attend church, the answers would vary greatly. Some come to serve. Some come for specific ministries or for preaching. Others come to gain respect or out of life's desperation. If you asked the same people to describe the purpose of the church, they might give reasonable answers, but their behavior suggests something else. Lots of people parrot reasonable statements about the nature and purpose of the church, but just watch to see what upsets them about their church. See where they actually make their demands or spend their time, and you might find out that many have no real understanding of what a church is and why it exists.

Every church needs a focus. And not just any focus—a kingdom *focus.* Some churches have a growth focus. Some have a seeker focus.

Others have a worship focus. Some have a pastor focus. The list of focus choices is endless: evangelism, missions, ministry, social causes, and so on. But how many have a kingdom focus? Without it, the key ingredients of what the Lord wants for churches will be absent, and the frustrations will build and build. Changing pastors, pastors changing churches, changing programs, methods, and adding "stuff" only makes things worse.

A kingdom-focused church is clear on two points: stewardship and ministry. Stewardship is vertical in the sense that a local church is under the authority and commission of the Father. It is His will, His truth, and His work that we do. We focus on Him; we serve Him and not ourselves. Ministry is horizontal in the sense that a church focuses on people. A pastor focuses not on himself but on his stewardship under God to serve his people. He preaches God's Word to God's people. He equips God's people for God's work. He takes God's gospel to the people in his community. It is about Him (God) and them (God's people).

A true *focus* begins with God and moves to people whom God loves and desires to be in relationship with Him. Methods, programs, worship services, events, activities, and the like all come *after* a kingdom focus in a church. Only with this order of focus will other priorities and programs be successful.

I once pastored a church with a swimming pool. That's right, a swimming pool—fully equipped with diving boards, dressing rooms, pool furniture, and picnic tables. Churches are known for a variety of things, but we could proudly boast that we were the only church for hundreds of miles around with a swimming pool.

Several things bothered me about this particular distinction. First, I can honestly say that if the decision were mine alone, no church would ever have a pool. Somehow I can always find more enjoyable or constructive things to do than swim. Next, if you own a pool, there are issues that some people never think about: liability, maintenance costs, personnel expenses, and the little matter of customer satisfaction. Then there are all the rules you need to run a pool efficiently.

The issues sound simple enough if you own a pool yourself or if you run a community pool as a public service. But think about it with me for a moment. Who owns a church pool? Who are the customers? Who should be able to use it? Should you charge church members and visitors for using the pool? If you do, are there implications for your church's tax-exempt status? How much value to the Great Commission is a church pool? Well, you get the picture.

In any church, whatever program or priority you have out there on the fringes of the Great Commission often becomes the center of controversy. For me all these questions came bearing down at once. It started when the recreation committee informed me that our pool was leaking water to the tune of three thousand dollars each month. I'm only a preacher, but I know that's a serious problem even for an Olympic-size pool, which is what we had. We met and decided that the pool should be closed "until further notice."

What I never could have imagined was that "further notice" would come in the form of a hastily called meeting with some concerned members. They requested my presence, complete with explanations of why the pool was now closed. I was surprised to see who came. Some were our best swimmers and most regular sunbathers, but I must admit the majority were members who never even used the pool. The meeting turned hostile, and I found myself defending something I really cared little about. The pool had been no big deal to me, but the controversy over its closing had now become mine to handle.

One evening a deacon—whom I love and trust to this very day—and I went visiting. As we left a home on our way back to the church, I brought up the pool controversy. He said something in his simple and direct way that I can never forget. He said, "Preacher, if I were you, I would leave that whole pool issue alone. Let the committee take care of it and get out of their way."

I thought about what he was saying, and it made perfect sense. Not every problem a pastor has is really "his" problem. I was focusing on something that wasn't really important, had nothing to do with my call to preach, and distracted me from the real job I should have been doing.

You and your church need a kingdom *focus*. You need to understand what the kingdom of God is and how you should live, lead, work, preach, and teach because of it. If you have never understood the importance of the kingdom of God in the life and teachings of the Lord, then I urge you to stop everything and begin an incredible journey through Scripture to find out its meaning for your life and work.

I see many pastors and church leaders who have replaced God's kingdom agenda with their own, and this is devastating. I know because for many years I pastored churches with my own agendas. Church growth methods, end-time speculations, programs, social causes, and political issues are important, but they are nothing compared to God's kingdom and His reign in this world today. In many churches God is pushed aside as we seek to build our churches, our lives, and even our own little personal kingdoms. I have written this before, but I want to say again, "Anything that starts with or centers in man will never focus on the kingdom of God."[1]

Many fine resources are available to the pastor and the church today. We have the finest seminaries around the world, books, conferences, and pastors who are leading some of the most exciting churches in history. There are resources that speak to the nature of the church in the twenty-first century; there are scientific studies, demographic studies, opinion polls, and other such resources as never before.

I would hasten to add, however, that most of these resources do not speak to the difficulty of fixing what is broken in congregations across the world. We speak of methods, purpose statements, discipleship plans, evangelism strategies, social connections with those in our cultures, and such things as these. But we continue to ignore the real issue of what defines our existence on earth as believers.

Think about it with me for a moment. What is *the* issue on earth today? If you had to boil everything down to one fundamental issue, what would you say that issue is?

Is it the global economy? Is it education? Is it peace? Is it justice? Is it church growth? Is it the nature of biblical inspiration? Is it the person of Christ?

How you answer that question will determine everything about your personal life, your family and marriage, your career, and your future. But what it will especially define is your church. The central issue in the world today is the advancement of the kingdom of God through kingdom communities we call churches.

Many times Christ expressed the pressing theological issue for every age. He did not make the church the central issue. He did not make the believer's personal experience the central issue. He did not make comfort, prosperity, health, peace, education, or religion His central focus.

Read His words below and see if you can guess the central issue of our age.

The Son of Man did not come to be served, but to serve, and to give His life—a ransom for many (Matt. 20:28).

For the Son of Man has come to seek and to save the lost (Luke 19:10).

For God loved the world in this way: He gave His only Son, so that everyone who believes in Him will not perish but have eternal life. For God did not send His Son into the world that He might judge the world, but that the world might be saved through Him (John 3:16–17).

Come to Me, all you who are weary and burdened, and I will give you rest (Matt. 11:28).

It's simple really. God created us and gave us incredible lives to live and enjoy. Our sin ruined His perfect gift, and we have no way to get it back except through Jesus Christ. Everything necessary for our restoration and redemption has been accomplished in Christ. There is nothing else to be done throughout the universe. What is left is the Great Commission.

Jesus' focus was clear. *The central issue in the universe was the salvation of all those living on earth in any generation.* It is the reason He came, and it is the reason He has given us the Great Commission. Bringing people into the kingdom must be our *focus* above anything else. We must be evangelists for Jesus Christ. People around the world live under the domination of Satan, the influence of the system of the world without Christ in their cultures, and the destruction of their own unbridled lusts of the flesh and mind. *And it is from this single issue that the local church must take its cue to its own nature and purpose.* This is also where we must look in order to "fix" those congregations that are now broken.

We can write books on better church practices, educate men and women who serve the body of Christ in various ministries, call upon pastors to be men of God and great leaders, and study denominations all we want. But until we know the real issue in our world and take that issue seriously, we will never build, start, or fix congregations. If we fail in this, we fail to fulfill the Great Commission, and our people will be forever wounded warriors who will never know the power of the resurrection of Christ as He intends.

The church started upon the Great Commission. The Lord said, "I want you to go and do one thing—make disciples." The command is to go, so we know the number one priority of a local church. It is to fulfill the Great Commission. And the number one priority in fulfilling the Great Commission is to be evangelistic. Most churches in the evangelical world do not have this as the only priority. That's why they fret about swimming pools.

It's so easy to do good things and forget the *one* thing that God has told us to do. Most of the time you can put your finger on the pulse of a church to see what's wrong. The staff does ministry inside the church, and that's about as far as it goes. And so we develop a whole generation of folks who are taught to sit and soak while staff members and a few key leaders sweat and strain trying to minister.

This is a case of the wrong people doing the right things at the wrong place. We come to church for training, equipping, and worshiping. We come to build relationships. We come sometimes because we are sin sick or soul sick or fainthearted, and we come to be ministered to and lifted up so we can go right back out there and do the Great Commission. When you start evaluating your church, don't look at the number of baptisms; look at the people who are being equipped to change the world in the places where they live and play and work and shop and travel.

I do not know of any church health issue that evangelism does not address. In fact, our current problems center on the fact that many of our congregations have turned aside from this priority to do any number of other things. And there are many good things to do in a local church. There are many fine ministries and fine programs. But nothing can substitute for or replace evangelism.

In the 1970s evangelical churches seemed strong and on the rise even in the face of secularism. Today evil is on the rise throughout the world, and congregations seem to be at a loss as to what to do about it. The strength we built in the sixties and seventies has evaporated. The twenty-first century opened with serious challenges for us and our churches, including:

- Modernism/postmodernism, which claim that there is no absolute truth and no true human nature
- Islam, a religion of revenge and retribution that is the fastest growing faith in the West
- Cultural Christianity, which Paul described perfectly in 2 Timothy 3:5 as "holding to the form of religion but denying its power."

If the church has lost its focus, we don't have anyone to blame but ourselves. When we lost the priority of evangelism in our churches, we lost the effectiveness of being salt and light to our world. We haven't been trained or challenged or led to be salt and light.

People sit around praying for revival. We also ought to pray for the training of faithful witnesses who will get out there and be salt and light. Pray that we will be ready to share this wonderful gospel.

You and I need three things in our lives that are important if we are to maintain kingdom *focus,* to grow in Christ, and, most important, to be effective as His ministers in this world. Jesus presents these essentials in the Gospel of John. If you understand them in your own life, you'll always know you're in right relationship to God. Whatever your dreams and circumstances are and however successful or unsuccessful you've been, when these three things are present in your life, you'll always have the balance you need. When they are present in the church, then we can really be the church that fulfills the Great Commission. And we will see people coming to completeness in Jesus Christ.

The first essential is faith or trust. In John 14:1, Jesus said, "Your heart must not be troubled. Believe in God; believe also in Me." That's the call of the ages. "For God loved the world in this way: He gave His only Son, so that everyone who believes in Him will not perish but have eternal life" (John 3:16).

Belief in Him starts with faith. Your faith in and of itself is of no value. Faith always starts with an object. If you put your faith in the church, you are in trouble. If you have put your faith in a pastor, you are in trouble. If you put your faith in a denomination, you are in trouble. If you have put your faith in this nation, you are in big trouble because this nation isn't consistent. Likewise, a pastor is not going to be consistent enough, and a church or denomination won't be consistent enough to take you through the muddy waters where life really happens. We all have been disappointed in people and programs and events and organizations. But the Lord said, "Believe in God; believe also in Me" (John 14:1). Faith starts it all.

What is the opposite of faith or trust? Fear. I guarantee you if you and I talked together one-on-one, sooner or later we would uncover fear in our lives. Fear is always the antithesis of faith. Fear is the great tool of the enemy. The world attacks us for who we are in Christ, and we begin to be afraid. We are afraid of the future. We are afraid to fly and afraid to eat. We are afraid of all of these things and more! Fear rises up, and there is no faith in our lives because we have quit trusting in Jesus Christ. We fear evangelizing lost people. We are bogged down. We are right where the enemy wants us. We have fear that is deep within, and we don't know how to handle it. The only way to handle it is by trusting in Christ. A disciple cannot live a life of fear.

The second essential Jesus talks about is love. In John 15, Jesus said: "Just as the Father has loved Me, I also have loved you. Remain in My love. . . . This is My commandment: that you love one another just as I have loved you. No one has greater love than this, that someone would lay down his life for his friends" (John 15:9,12–13).

Our world is inundated with cliches about love. Genuine love, however, always compels us to action. Those actions, motivated by love, can make the message irresistible to a hurting and often aimless world. Jesus said, "By this all people will know that you are My disciples, if you have love for one another" (John 13:35).

Galatians 5:22–23 says, "The fruit of the Spirit is love, joy, peace, patience, kindness, goodness, faith, gentleness, self-control. Against such things there is no law." The fruit of the Spirit means the absence of the works of the flesh or the dependency on the flesh—which can destroy us. No gift of the Holy Spirit is going to be used effectively without love. If a church doesn't have love but has the best preacher, the best leaders, and the best whatever else you want, it will be for nothing because the fruit of the Spirit is not being manifested.

God puts us in relationship with Him by the presence of the Holy Spirit, and He bears fruit in our lives so that we can love one another. Listen, we don't all agree with one another. If we spent enough time together, you and I would disagree over something. We might hope to agree on everything, but eventually we would disagree on something. We don't have the same opinions, background, or orientation. God, of course, was undeterred by this, knowing that our life experiences were no match for the presence of the Holy Spirit leading us to love one another. "Dear friends, let us love one another, because love is from God, and everyone who loves has been born of God and knows God. The one who does not love does not know God, because God is love" (1 John 4:7–8).

Love for one another. Every church has it and every church needs it.

The third essential, Jesus says, is that we have to keep His Word, to obey Him. Your Christian life revolves around faith, love, and obedience. When you've got those covered, you are going to be all right. Jesus said, "If you love Me, you will keep My commandments" (John 14:15). He added, "If you keep My commandments you will remain in My love, just as I have kept My Father's commandments and remain in His love" (John 15:10). Dallas Willard wrote well in his book *Renovation of the Heart,* when he stated, "Obedience is an eventual outcome of Christian spiritual formation."[2]

Why did God command us to do certain things like being obedient? Do you think it was so we could scratch our heads and think about it? When He commands us to be holy or to go and make disciples or to be kind to one another, did He do that because He wanted us to stop and consider and muse about it a while? No. It was because He wants us to follow Him and to do whatever He commands.

There are a lot of times when my "love tank" in a church begins to drain out a little bit. You know, you just get tired of it all. Do you ever get tired of your family? Sure. You kind of rub each other the wrong way sometimes. That's the way it is in relationships. When my love tank goes down, it doesn't mean my obedience has to go out the window. It doesn't mean my faith staggers. When my unbelief begins to rise and fear begins to take its place, it doesn't mean that I am excused from obeying the Lord.

I like what one preacher said. He said we are used to singing the song, "Trust and Obey." But when you can't trust Him, you still have to obey Him. I like that. We still walk in holiness. When my obedience tank is kind of dragging along, it doesn't mean I am free not to love people. The opposite of faith is fear. What's the opposite of love? Most of us would say hate. That's not the opposite of love; the opposite of love is selfishness.

I always know when my love tank is going down because I get to thinking about me more and more. I want me and my demands and what I need and how I understand it. It's a plague to the church whenever that starts happening. Selfishness is the root of all sin. The sin of independence, the sin of self-gratification, self-glorification. What's the opposite of obedience? Rebellion. It's not just disobedience; it's absolute rebellion against God.

Selfishness also leads me to focus on me and not on the first work of the church. *Focus*—real, steady, dedicated focus on the Great Commission to evangelize and spread the gospel—is hard to maintain. You've got to keep after it all the time, constantly fine-tuning and moving forward. But your reward is a church that invests its energy and resources in work that works, rather than drifting away sooner or later into frustration and failure.

So spiritual focus boils down to faith, love, and obedience. From the *focus* on evangelism comes the *focus* on spiritual transformation. Making disciples always comes first. Maturing believers always follows. No options. No debate. Building their lives into Christ, then multiplying their lives in ministry is the church's kingdom *focus.*

To have a focus is to see the right things clearly and then to act on those things. *The* church you lead must have the right *focus* and that is a *kingdom* focus. It must focus on the King and His agenda. It must understand Him, experience Him, and then do what He commands.

Chapter 6

CHURCH—WHAT IT IS AND WHAT IT ISN'T

PASTOR MIKE HANGS UP THE PHONE and stares at his writing pad once again. He is beginning to see some of the problems with his approach and considers the frustration he's been feeling. As he muses and doodles with his pen, a question pops into his head.

"If a restaurant serves food to people, and a hotel provides rooms for people, what does a church do?" he asks. "What is a church and what does it do?"

That question is the central question—*the* question for every pastor everywhere. If we don't answer that question, then we can never know if what we are doing is right or not. Without the answer, we cannot have a proper focus or a kingdom view of the things that we experience each day. Mike may not know it now, but he is beginning to take great steps toward becoming an awesome pastor. Sometimes it just takes a combination of failure, frustration, and humility to break through to becoming an effective kingdom leader. One of the best results is that his church and his people will benefit greatly from what he is on the verge of discovering.

One of the great problems in churches today is that too few people see the ultimate reason for their existence. It's not surprising, then, that people come and go, leaders come and go, and churches come and go without ever realizing what is crucial and thus what is keeping them from success.

A local church is a unique body of believers in a specific location somewhere in the world. Each church is a part of the language, society, culture, and geography of its environment. The customs, beliefs, experiences, and history of the people in any given region all have an influence on a local church. As a result, local churches are shaped and influenced by these factors, and this makes them different in different countries and locations. That, in turn, is what makes the local church one of God's mightiest tools. But for God to reach every person, He must work through believers who live with and near them.

A local church exists to reach people for Christ in a given location. Its primary responsibility is to reach the people God has placed near that local congregation. Size is never the issue here. The issue is not how many members there are but how willing those members are to see the real issue—eternal life for those who do not know Christ and are separated from Him.

I want to be deliberate here because to miss this truth in our definition is to miss the heart and soul of who God is, what He is doing in Christ, and what the nature of a church truly is. Every body of believers we call a local church is a kingdom community where every believer is a part of the kingdom of God. The church exists expressly for the purpose of establishing God's kingdom, His rule and reign, in the lives of the people in the community where it thrives. A kingdom community—the local church—exists for much more than itself.

What exactly is a *church?* I like A. H. Strong's definition from his systematic theology written many years ago. In part, it reads:

The individual church may be defined as that
smaller company of regenerate persons, who, in any
given community, unite themselves voluntarily together,

in accordance with Christ's laws, for the purpose of
securing the complete establishment of his kingdom in
themselves and in the world.[1]

There are many other definitions too. And although I admire a number of them, I'm going to take the plunge here and suggest one of my own. I said it in a slightly different way in chapter 2, but I like this short, succinct statement.

A local *church* is a kingdom community of believers
in dynamic fellowship under Christ's lordship. Its purpose is to establish the kingdom as it fulfills the Great
Commission with a passion to see every person complete in Christ through making disciples, maturing
believers, and multiplying ministries.

We should never substitute the centrality of the kingdom of God and the kingdom agenda for another focus for our lives and our churches. It isn't appropriate for us to have individual, local church, or denominational agendas. There is only *one* agenda—and that *one* has been established and set in motion by the Father through the work of His Son. His agenda must be our only concern. That agenda is not something that exists in theory or as some abstract ideal. It is a real agenda for the redemption of everyone Christ died for, and we must give our lives to see that it is fulfilled. It is an agenda we individually fulfill in the context of a local church. The central thrust of God's kingdom agenda must come out of local churches, those kingdom communities intent on fulfilling the Great Commission with passion.

Let's look at the definition more closely for clarity and comment, keeping in mind that our source is always Scripture, and it is our authority for faith and practice.

A local *church* is a unit of believers who gather together in a specific location. In that location the believers who gather generally speak a common language, are influenced by a common culture, and often belong to the same ethnic or racial group either by birth or choice. Of course, there are many variations in the makeup of local churches, but generally they have these characteristics.

The kingdom of God has no geography, no social standing, no economic differences, no single culture, and no ethnic or racial groups. A local church, however, as a kingdom community must exist somewhere with some persons who belong to one another in it. A local church is not the kingdom of God, although it is a part of it.

Also, a local church is not "The Church." Some call "The Church" the "Universal Church," or, erroneously, the "Invisible Church." By "The Church" we mean all believers for all times—past, present, and future.

A local *church* is the gathering of believers to worship and serve the Lord in their own way and understanding of who He is and what He wants them to be and do.

In an earlier book, *The 7 Churches NOT in the Book of Revelation,*[2] I wrote about the different kinds of local churches that developed in particular communities, depending on the membership and the environment. Once established, churches of a particular type tend to attract new members that share their characteristics. They are:

- The University Church—where the emphasis is on teaching, learning, and doctrine
- The Arena Church—worship centered, where performance and entertainment are key
- The Corporate Church—large, complex, efficient, and focused on a vision
- The Machine Church—program oriented; focused on building, missions, and task management
- The Family Chapel Church—based on family ties, where personal relationships come first

- The Legacy Church—rich in tradition, often focused on a great event or personality of the past
- The Community Center Church—committed to community service and local issues

Whatever kind of church you're in, you're part of a body of like-minded believers. It's interesting that we speak of a church as a "body." When you think of a human body, you probably think of its functions: cardiovascular, respiratory, neurological, and others. Functions reveal tasks that are important to the body.

A *church* likewise can be described as a body with certain parts doing certain tasks. There are individuals in every local church who have spiritual gifts to be used within the body. We use those gifts to minister to other parts of the body so that it can be built up, sustained, and kept healthy.

The Holy Spirit produces the fruit of the Spirit in order to allow good relationships, which allows those in the church to use their spiritual gifts effectively. Think about spiritual fruit and spiritual gifts for a moment. Every fruit is relational, and every gift is functional.

But the fruit of the Spirit is love, joy, peace, patience,
kindness, goodness, faith, gentleness, self-control.
Against such things there is no law (Gal. 5:22–23).

You may have never noticed that each fruit enables us to have good relationships with one another. Since the fruit of the Spirit is relational, there is not a gift here; there is not a task. There is nothing you do with the fruit of the Spirit. The fruit of the Spirit is critical because without it kingdom relationships are impossible. The presence of the fruit of the Spirit creates an environment where spiritual gifts can flourish.

If I speak the languages of men and of angels,
but do not have love,
I am a sounding gong or a clanging cymbal.

If I have the gift of prophecy,
and understand all mysteries and all knowledge,
and if I have all faith,
so that I can move mountains,
but do not have love,
I am nothing.
And if I donate all my goods to feed the poor,
and if I give my body to be burned,
but do not have love,
I gain nothing.
Love is patient; love is kind.
Love does not envy;
is not boastful; is not conceited (1 Cor. 13:1–4).
According to the grace given to us, we have different
gifts:
If prophecy, use it according to the standard of faith;
if service, in service;
if teaching, in teaching;
if exhorting, in exhortation;
giving, with generosity;
leading, with diligence;
showing mercy, with cheerfulness.
Love must be without hypocrisy. . . . Show family
affection to one another with brotherly love (Rom.
12:6–10).

Now the end of all things is near; therefore, be clear-
headed and disciplined for prayer. Above all, keep your
love for one another at full strength, since love covers a
multitude of sins. Be hospitable to one another without
complaining. Based on the gift they have received,
everyone should use it to serve others, as good managers

of the varied grace of God. If anyone speaks, his speech
should be like the oracles of God; if anyone serves, his
service should be from the strength God provides, so
that in everything God may be glorified through Jesus
Christ. To Him belong the glory and the power forever
and ever. Amen! (1 Pet. 4:7–11).

Do you see in these passages the unmistakable relationship of the
fruit of the Spirit and spiritual gifts in believers' lives? It is unfortu-
nate when believers seek only to discover and use their spiritual gifts
without understanding the necessary work of the Holy Spirit that
enables them to be in good relationship with fellow believers. God
produces spiritual fruit in our lives which, combined with spiritual
gifts, is how church work gets done.

We have to understand the essential task of building and main-
taining healthy relationships within a local church. While these relationships don't take the place of our individual relationship with the
Father, they are His will for us. It is His will that we belong to Him
as we belong to one another. It is His will that we love one another in
order to serve one another.

Our first relationship as a *church,* then, is with God in Christ as
part of the kingdom. Our second relationship is with other believers
in our church. The third relationship we have is with unbelievers. To
ignore building relationships with the lost around us is to ignore the
Great Commission. As we saw in looking at the *focus* of a church in
the last chapter, the Great Commission is the key to understanding
what God is doing in our world at this moment. The central issue in
the universe today is the redemption of persons separated from God.
He is bringing people back to Himself in great numbers each day, and
He does so by using the church as His redemptive agent.

You cannot understand your life apart from an understanding of
the Lord and His love for you. Likewise, you can't understand your

Christian life if you don't understand God's will for you to witness to those around you. He has placed you in their lives for this purpose, and your Christian life and your church's life will never be complete until you understand this and actively become a consistent witness to the lost. Remember that *the first priority of a local church must be evangelism.* The mandate for evangelism is clear in Scripture. The salvation of people around the world is the only way to transform societies and cultures. The only way for your church and mine to grow is through evangelism.

Whatever we decide about the condition of our churches, we must not forget that God has placed them in specific locations in His world. We may be in emerging neighborhoods or declining ones, but we are in communities of people searching for the answers that we alone have. We may like where we are or fear where we are, but we are where we are! Local churches are just that. They are congregations of believers who exist to meet the central issue in our universe today, namely that people who are lost in their sins are within reach of God's mercy, grace, and salvation. His kingdom is near, and they can be redeemed from the curse of their sins.

What about parachurch organizations? To me these are groups that focus on specific kingdom agendas. They may focus on family, students, professionals, or athletes. They may focus on discipleship, evangelism, or even worship. They focus on a part of the local church's assignment, but they never focus on all of it. As much good as they do, they can never replace local churches and their mission.

Some say that parachurch organizations exist to strengthen what local churches have ignored. If this is true, leaders of these local churches should work to strengthen whatever is lacking. You cannot replace what God has set in place. In reality, many parachurch organizations do help individual believers, but their role is not to strengthen local churches.

The strength of local churches is that they have the opportunity to fulfill the Great Commission in a local setting. The Great Commission begins somewhere and ends everywhere, so there is logic in what we are assigned to do. We are to reach people for Christ wherever our churches are located. The community where your church is located is the mission field God has given you. Don't worry about its demographics. Don't worry about the crime rate, the average annual income of its people, or whether its streets are smooth and tree-lined avenues of comfort and security. Your reason for being where you are is to reach the people around you. In times past we thought of areas around churches as "church fields." Today we are more urban and mobile, and so distance to and from church is no longer a great factor people use to determine whether they will attend your church. But while distance is not a great factor, proximity is a great factor in fulfilling the Great Commission. We gather in specific locations to reach all those in and around those locations.

Do not be fooled into believing that you can be a city or regional church and not reach those around you. If they are of a different race, language, or culture, your responsibility under Christ's lordship is to overcome those barriers in order to evangelize them and minister to their needs. They are in your kingdom responsibility, and you must lead your people to see it and then to meet it. Don't move away; move out to reach them.

We live in a time of great self-interest and great selfishness. We are taught to be self-supporting, self-reliant, self-guided from the time of our birth. It is a part of the American culture to privatize everything we can, including our beliefs and the ways we practice them. We are encouraged to tolerate the beliefs of others and to support them in their right to believe or not to believe anything they choose. I would never deny a person the right to believe or not believe anything, but that does not excuse in any way my own responsibility to live under the Lord's authority and share the gospel with every person I can.

All the cultural restrictions guarding our privacy notwithstanding, you and I are here to make disciples—period. Our churches are here to make disciples—period. If it is hard, so be it. If it goes against our culture, too bad. Whether things are easy or hard for us, we have the responsibility to obey God's commands.

The kingdom of God is the beauty of all that we have in Christ. It is beautiful and perfect in every dimension. The *church*, however, is a kingdom community in a broken world. It is the place where believers gather in the middle of real life. It is a community of Christians in communities of sinful persons. Churches exist in the dirt and filth of broken lives and lustful people. They are built in the face of opposition to bear the gospel to those who need the Lord but do not want Him.

A local *church* is the intersection of the kingdom and your community, the future and the present. It is a place where the Lord is worshiped and the lost are reached. It is where God, through His people, invades life on earth. It is where Christ comes to invade the indolence of prosperity and the cries of poverty. It is where He announces the end to the slavery of sin and the struggles of failure. It is where He meets us at the point of our need and comforts us at the point of our fear.

The *church* you lead is a kingdom agent, placed there at the will of God to be salt and light to people without a clue or a hope. It is a dynamic body of believers who exist to exalt the Lord and labor for His causes. It is a family of God building relationships among people and pointing them to the Heavenly Father.

The kingdom has always been and never changes, but the *church* is dynamic and is always changing. The kingdom is universal, and the *church* is first and foremost local, geographical. Churches are a part of their cultures, colored by languages, races, and social standings. The kingdom transcends all these characteristics. The kingdom of God contains the church, and churches exist on behalf of the kingdom of God.

To be a kingdom-focused *church,* we must remove false notions and unclear understanding about what a local church is. It is an outpost in a war zone where real life happens. It is not a fortress to hide in or a pristine edifice to impress those who pass its doors. No, a church is a gathering of real people, living real lives, struggling with real issues. It is a place on earth where pilgrims on a journey make their way to eternity. It is a place where every imaginable struggle occurs and every sin is sinned. It is a place of transformation and miracles. It is a place where God surprises us in unexpected, unpredictable, and unknowable ways.

We need pastors and church leaders who understand what a church is and who are willing to work to see that their church becomes what God desires. We need men of God who lead the people of God to accomplish the will of God in their communities. We need churches with a kingdom focus and nothing less.

God has called you to the essential work of leading His people. You feel that calling, or else you wouldn't have read this far. Don't give up or give out. Get your focus, and then get your church to focus itself on becoming and being what God demands. It's all yours for the taking. Now I invite you to read on and see what specifically you can do to make your church *the kingdom-focused church.*

Chapter 7

HOW A KINGDOM-FOCUSED CHURCH WORKS

I F MIKE IS GOING TO BE ABLE TO LEAD HIS CHURCH and bring about the focus it needs, he will need more than a manual for leading a perfect church. His experience, like that of the Formula One rookie driver, must go beyond the ability to drive. He must not only preach, teach, and pastor; he must also lead his people to become what God intends them to be. He has asked the right question about the nature of the church. Once he understands the true nature of a church as a dynamic fellowship of believers, he must move quickly to a knowledge of how it works.

In other words, he must be able to put into practical application what he has learned. He must successfully combine a kingdom focus with a kingdom strategy. Learning how a church works is a key step to success as a leader. Fortunately for our young pastor, he has to go no further than the Bible for his help. The Bible, especially the New Testament, is a living record of the nature of the local church and the principles of how it grows to health and effectiveness.

Now that we've seen what a kingdom-focused church is, let's take a look at how it works. The New Testament tells us there are five functions every church needs to do in order to fulfill the Great

Commission. That means, regardless of the variables in community type, ethnic makeup, financial condition, and all the rest, these five interrelated functions are essential for establishing and holding a kingdom focus and becoming a successful church.

These aren't new functions. In fact, they're old and familiar, far more ordinary than innovative, and you've probably heard them a million times. However, if you look honestly and carefully at your church, you may discover that you are putting only one or two of them into practice. They're easy to understand and talk about but hard to do, and even harder to commit to for the long term. But they're what you have to do to build a kingdom-focused church.

Before you can apply them to your church, you have to apply them to yourself. These functions can only be infused into a church by people who have them solidly within their own hearts first. If you sit around complaining, waiting for somebody else to get busy and bring these functions to your congregation, you'll wait forever, and your church will never achieve what it could.

The five functions of every kingdom-focused church are described in Acts 2 as part of the response to Peter's sermon on the day of Pentecost. This is when it was explained in detail for the first time how the church would grow and the gospel message would spread through the disciples and other Christian followers after Jesus' death. Together the five functions lead directly to an effective, powerful, kingdom-focused church.

Evangelism

Christian evangelism is the process of sharing the gospel with the lost and winning them to Christ, thereby enabling them to enter the kingdom of God. It is asking them to repent of their sins, put their faith in Christ for the forgiveness of sins and the gift of eternal life, and to follow Him forever as Lord. Evangelism is the good news spoken by believers and lived out in their lives.

Peter described the process of evangelism to his listeners in Acts 2:38–41:

> "Repent," Peter said to them, "and be baptized, each of you, in the name of Jesus the Messiah for the forgiveness of your sins, and you will receive the gift of the Holy Spirit. For the promise is for you and for your children, and for all who are far off, as many as the Lord our God will call." And with many other words he testified and strongly urged them, saying, "Be saved from this corrupt generation!"
>
> So those who accepted his message were baptized, and that day about 3,000 people were added to them.

As we've seen already, evangelism is the ultimate goal of the kingdom-focused church, and everything the church does has to contribute one way or another to reaching that goal. It's also true that church growth without evangelism is impossible. No minister, believer, or church can say they believe salvation is possible only through the grace of Jesus Christ and then not share that news with the world at every opportunity.

The heart of evangelism is the good news of the kingdom of God. In the Old Testament the good news is seen in God's calling out His chosen people Israel, redeeming them from Egyptian slavery, and later, Babylonian exile. In the New Testament God's good news is seen in Jesus. Early believers considered it a responsibility and a privilege to share the message of salvation. Persecution and fear could not stop them or lessen their God-given power.

There are all kinds of ways to evangelize. The best method for you and your church may be different from the next church down the street or your denominational cousin in another city. You may prefer to establish friendships with people before you witness to them, while someone else is comfortable approaching a total stranger. However you want to do it, sharing the gospel with every person as soon as possible is the task God has given His people. The methods you use are important, but not as important as the effort and the ultimate result.

Unfortunately, we're too quick to discuss and argue about methodology while the unsaved perish all around us. The *how* should never take the place of the *why.*

God saves us and uses us to deliver His message of salvation to others. God's mission is to redeem sinners from their sin, and His method for doing that is to use you and me to share the redemptive Word and carry out the ministry of redemption in the world.

As the world grows more populated, it seems that more and more Christians and churches practice less and less evangelism. Evangelism can change the world for good. Just look at the work of great reformers like John Calvin, Martin Luther, and John and Charles Wesley. Their evangelistic zeal ultimately transformed entire nations and cultures. Ignoring an opportunity to evangelize can change the course of history for the worse as much as action in the name of Christ can change it for the better.

After Marco Polo returned from the magnificent imperial court of Kublai Khan in 1296, he wrote that the mighty Khan asked him to request that the Pope send him a hundred priests to teach Christianity to his subjects. Then, according to Polo, Kublai Khan said, "I shall allow myself to be baptized. Following my example, all my nobility will then in like manner receive baptism, and this will be imitated by my subjects in general. In the end the Christians of these parts will exceed in number those who inhabit your own country."

Polo concluded, "From this discourse it must be evident that if the Pope had sent out persons duly qualified to preach the gospel, the

Great Khan would have embraced Christianity, for which, it is certainly known, he had a strong predilection."

The Pope could spare only two friars for the evangelization of China, both of whom turned back before they were halfway there, saying the trip was too difficult. Imagine how different the world would be today if Kublai Khan's invitation had been accepted!

As a sinner redeemed by the blood of Christ, you have a responsibility to share the good news with those who have never responded or never heard it. You know what it's like to be saved, to be softened through the convicting power of the Holy Spirit to receive the gospel. You know how it feels to repent, place your trust in Christ, and live your life as a forgiven child of the covenant. That's a feeling even the angels have never experienced!

Evangelism is essential in the kingdom-focused church. It is a sign that the church leaders and members are spiritually sound. It is a sign the church is alive and healthy. It produces new converts, a new generation of believers to carry God's message forward.

Discipleship

Though it's very familiar and often discussed, discipleship is probably the weakest and least practiced function in the church. Discipleship is a lifelong journey of obedience to Christ that transforms a person's values and behavior and results in ministry in one's home, church, and the world. Discipling is the process of teaching the new citizens in the kingdom of God to love, trust, and obey Him, and teach them how to win and train others to do the same.

Luke describes discipleship in Acts 2:42–43:

They devoted themselves to the apostles' teaching, to fellowship, to the breaking of bread, and to prayers. Then fear came over everyone, and many wonders and signs were being performed through the apostles.

There's a tremendous interest in discipleship, as shown by the large and ever-growing number of seminars, books, conferences, and articles about the subject. Church members and leaders are genuinely interested in it and evidently recognize its importance. Unfortunately, there's often more talk than action because discipleship means complete transformation. It calls for undivided attention and total commitment from church leaders and members.

Discipleship is a demanding discipline; it's not an option. Paul discusses it in detail in Ephesians, describing those who labor "for the training of the saints in the work of ministry, to build up the body of Christ" (Eph. 4:12). Jesus mandates it in the Great Commission, "teaching them to observe everything I have commanded you" (Matt. 28:20). He also reminded those who would be His disciples that they must be willing to sacrifice.

If anyone wants to come with Me, he must deny himself, take up his cross daily, and follow Me. For whoever wants to save his life will lose it, but whoever loses his life because of Me will save it (Luke 9:23–24).

In a culture where some people tend to gloss over serious matters, discipleship requires a dedication and intensity many people don't understand. To understand that discipleship is not an option for believers and that it involves taking up your cross daily to follow Christ is the beginning of understanding the work of every believer and every congregation.

Discipleship is a necessary function of the kingdom-focused church. Church members and leaders draw closer to Christ as they immerse themselves in His service. As believers become more like Christ, their lives move closer to the uncompromised perfection of Christ's example.

The idea of discipleship isn't put into practice very much because it goes against the grain of contemporary culture. Today we're bombarded by the message that the only thing that matters in life is the individual; it's every man for himself. Be selfish, do what you have to do to get ahead—hey, you're worth it! This is exactly the opposite of what happens to disciples. The life of a disciple is one of struggle, danger, inconvenience, and sometimes terrible suffering. All but one of the twelve apostles met violent deaths as a result of their work, some of them almost too grisly to imagine: stoning, upside-down crucifixion, being skinned alive.

I don't expect any of us will undergo such horrible treatment. But the lesson here is that nothing about the Christian life is natural or easy, and discipling others is the hardest task the church has to do. We are to give our lives to world evangelism and to discipling believers. We have no greater commitment to God than to be willing to go anywhere to fulfill His mission of world redemption through evangelism and discipleship.

Fellowship

Fellowship is more than just a feeling of goodwill in a congregation. It is a result of the intimate spiritual relationship that Christians share with God and other believers through their relationship with Jesus Christ. Fellowship doesn't evolve naturally in a community of believers but comes only by the power of God working through and among them.

The Bible describes the days after Pentecost this way:

And they devoted themselves to the apostles' teaching, to fellowship, to the breaking of bread, and to prayers. . . . And every day they devoted themselves to meeting together in the temple complex, and broke

bread from house to house. They ate their food with
gladness and simplicity of heart, praising God and having favor with all the people (Acts 2:42, 46–47).

After the coming of the Holy Spirit at Pentecost, a unique fellowship came together. The followers of Jesus began sharing meals
with one another and worshiping together in friendship and
mutual support. Of all the activities Christ could have chosen
to symbolize His relationship with mankind, He chose a
meal. Clearly there's the symbol of feeding, strengthening, and
nurturing His people spiritually, pouring His perfection into their
imperfect vessels. But equally important is the idea of fellowship.
Communion is a shared experience.

When Christians try to celebrate the Lord's Supper as anything
besides a fellowship of believers, it's a sign that their faith and their
church are both in trouble. Paul warned the Corinthian church that
they were endangering the church's welfare by abusing the Lord's
Supper on account of their divisions, disputes, and selfishness. He
warned them that a church in their condition shouldn't even participate in so holy an act. He warned those early believers that such crude
violations could result in disaster for the church.

So a man should examine himself; in this way he
should eat of the bread and drink of the cup. For whoever eats and drinks without recognizing the body, eats
and drinks judgment on himself. This is why many are
sick and ill among you, and many have fallen asleep
(1 Cor. 11:28–30).

Without warm, loving fellowship no church can grow. People will
never feel welcome in a place where bickering, selfishness, coldness,
and tension hang heavy in the air. Fellowship must follow evangelism
and discipleship to make a place in the church where new Christians
feel at home. When church fellowship is broken, you can be sure that

other characteristics of a kingdom-focused church are missing or in tatters as well.

Ultimately the church is bound together not with creeds or confessions, not with programs and ministries, but with a unity produced by the Holy Spirit and driven by God's love for us and our love for Him and one another. The church is blessed with the ministry of the Holy Spirit convicting us of our sins and making us alive forever in Jesus. He produces spiritual fruit for us to build our lives together. If fellowship is missing, the Holy Spirit is not in charge. The transformation is from me, my, and mine to you, yours, and ours.

As well as being a product of the Holy Spirit, fellowship encourages churches to evangelize. The motivation to reach the lost is stimulated and heightened by a desire to bring them into fellowship with Christ and other Christians. Fellowship allows believers to experience the richness of human and divine relationships and points them to eternity when we will live together with Jesus forever. Fellowship enables us to experience God's family now and gives us a taste of what the family will be like in heaven.

Ministry

Ministry is meeting another person's need in the name of Jesus, expressed as service to people inside the church family and expressed as missions to those outside the church with the resources God provides. This ministry grows out of a transformed and serving life. It is probably the best understood and most faithfully practiced function.

Acts 2:44–45 describes it this way:

> Now all the believers were together and had everything in common. So they sold their possessions and property and distributed the proceeds to all, as anyone had a need.

Christian ministry is evangelistic by its very nature and helps believers mature in their faith. Jesus never separated doing good from doing God's will. Whatever good the early church accomplished was done in the name of Jesus and for God's glory. Believers best minister to others after they have embraced evangelism and discipleship. As Moses said in the familiar passage from Deuteronomy 8:3, "Man does not live on bread alone but on every word that comes from the mouth of the LORD" (NIV). A person's spiritual needs are more important than his physical needs.

There were times when God allowed the Israelites to go without food and water in the desert. This experience tested the people's loyalty and taught them the valuable lesson that spiritual food is more important than physical refreshment. Jesus reinforced this fundamental truth when He refused food during His temptation in the wilderness.

Ministry does not supersede evangelism but will always be part of a kingdom-focused church. Christian compassion demands that we minister to everyone regardless of race, religion, abilities, or circumstances. We must meet needs not as we see fit but in response to Jesus' teaching and example. As He reminded His disciples in Mark 14:7, "You always have the poor with you, and you can do good for them whenever you want, but you do not always have Me."

You and I must always be willing to minister to the poor by using the resources God provides. Human need around the world is so staggering that our own resources alone will never be enough to meet them. As God expects us to minister, He gives us the power and the means to do so. In fact, we have to minister in order to be good stewards of the faith and abilities God has given us.

Besides ministering to the world, we also have a right and obligation to minister within the church. All believers are gifted by the Holy Spirit to minister according to the will of God. Within the church body, ministry isn't just the responsibility of pastors and leaders but part of the spiritual expression and fulfillment of every believer.

We can't minister in isolation. Leaders who start describing their church as "my ministry" expose a dangerous misunderstanding of the nature of ministry. None of us owns the ministry God has blessed us with. We're only stewards of it. In fact, the very thought of "owning" a ministry scares me to death. There's no way I can meet the needs of everyone in a church I pastor or a ministry I conduct by myself. But working together with other believers and through the power of the Holy Spirit, I can meet those needs, both inside and outside the church. And the church will grow and prosper as it does the Lord's work.

Worship

Worship is any activity in which believers experience God in a meaningful, spiritually transforming way. It leads worshipers to a deeper appreciation for God, a better understanding of His ways, and a deeper commitment to Him. Worship brings us face-to-face with our Creator and draws us closer to His image.

As Acts 2:46–47 relates:

And every day they devoted themselves to meeting together in the temple complex, and broke bread from house to house. They ate their food with gladness and simplicity of heart, praising God and having favor with all the people. And every day the Lord added those being saved to them.

The most recognized and obvious act of worship is a church service. In the twenty-first century, worship has a wider range of meaning than ever before. We're in the midst of rediscovering and redefining contemporary worship. We have to be careful not to let genuine, heartfelt worship get lost in the glitz of popular entertainment. This isn't to say contemporary approaches to worship are wrong or that you shouldn't try new things. You can have an authentic worship experience that's pleasing to God whether your pulpit is pine or Plexiglas™. But the spirit of worship has to be there. Nothing about church today has been analyzed and changed and worried over as much as worship. However, true worship doesn't depend on form. Worship is only possible in a disciple's heart. How we live for Christ and how He transforms us daily is the key to worship. What we bring in is more central than what we leave with.

Effective worship meets the spiritual needs of believers while at the same time attracting and including unbelievers. It comes from the commands of God in Scripture and the grateful hearts of the redeemed, who long to come before the Lord to praise Him and acknowledge His presence in their lives.

While worship styles can be adjusted for personal, cultural, or practical reasons, the Bible gives us specific instructions about what all worship should be. God is in charge of worship, and He expects us to worship Him as He directs. Worship must be guided by leaders who are believers, have a kingdom focus, understand the culture and context of the worshipers, are themselves being transformed by the worship experience, and believe that God seeks those who worship Him in spirit and truth.

Old Testament worship tended to focus on celebrating religious festivals, the ark of the covenant, sacrifices, and the Sabbath. In the New Testament the emphasis clearly moves to a personal relationship with Christ and the indwelling of the Holy Spirit, giving Christians a new dimension in worship.

These five functions—evangelism, discipleship, fellowship, ministry, and worship—describe what the kingdom-focused church does. Together they give every church all it needs to grow and prosper in service to Christ. Now let's look at the results you can expect when your church uses these functions to enrich God's people.

Chapter 8

EXPERIENCING
KINGDOM RESULTS

A ND NOW COMES THE BIG MOMENT when Mike asks, "So where does all this get me? What happens to my church because it's a kingdom-focused church?"

The short answer is, "Good things, including growth in numbers." But the not-so-short answer is a lot more exciting, rewarding, and encouraging than that. It's only right that we should spend some time looking in detail at the results you can expect when you focus your church and your ministry on the Great Commission.

Jesus told us to "seek first the kingdom of God and His righteousness, and all these things will be provided for you" (Matt. 6:33). These days putting the kingdom first is a tall order. There are so many distractions and temptations that conspire to lure us toward some other goal that it's easy to get derailed. However, by obeying God in faith and seeking His kingdom first, you will see God build a church that meets other objectives too. A kingdom focus leads to kingdom results.

Bookstores and catalogs are full of resources promising to make your church grow. Private institutes, seminary centers, and denominational organizations do the same. A vast array of conferences, resources, workshops, consultants, and teaching organizations has sprung up all over the place. Emphasis on growth is fine, but as long as the pathway depends on methods and techniques, churches will fall short of their kingdom potential.

True church growth is never the result of methods. It is the result of the supernatural activity of God. Though many people associate church growth only with numerical increase, this idea is far too limiting. Churches exist in a cycle of birth, development, growth, plateau, decline, and sometimes death. Yet in spite of the rise and fall of an individual church, the kingdom of God never stops growing. Churches are living agents of kingdom growth, but not every church can grow numerically forever.

Growth in attendance or enrollment is the most obvious kind of growth a kingdom-focused church has and the one many preachers keep an eye on above all else. It's easy to let attendance serve as a marker of a pastor's success. (Let's be honest and admit a bigger audience means more bragging rights.) But the fact is there are four dimensions of growth in a kingdom-focused church, and true success can be measured only by considering them all: numerical growth, spiritual transformation, ministry expansion, and kingdom advance.

1. *Numerical growth* is simply God's increase of the church that can be measured in membership, in baptisms, and in worship and Bible study attendance.

2. *Spiritual transformation* is God's work of changing a believer into the likeness of Jesus, which is reflected in a lifelong relationship of love, faith, and obedience.

3. *Ministry expansion* occurs when believers are transformed spiritually and are given new ministry opportunities by the Holy Spirit.

4. *Kingdom advance* is God's constant work of expanding His kingdom through the local church as one person at a time around the world is reached for Christ.

Like the legs of a table, each of the four has to work in harmony with the other three to achieve the right result. One extra-long leg by itself won't make up for a deficit in the others. Beyond a certain point, concentrating on one kind of growth at the expense of the rest can actually do more harm than good. But if you're a kingdom-focused church, you will experience growth in all four areas according to God's perfect will.

I cannot give you the magnitude of the results or the order in which they will come. But I assure you they will come. Implementing the Great Commission through the five functions of the church (evangelism, discipleship, fellowship, ministry, and worship) ensures, guarantees, and determines (you get the picture) that you will experience *numerical, spiritual, ministry, and kingdom growth!* It is a kingdom law just as certain as gravity. Kingdom results are simply indications of the supernatural activity of God expressed in, through, and around God's people in local churches. God's activity transforms the lives of His people as He uses them to accomplish His purposes for His glory around the world.

Numerical Growth

Through His churches God gathers a harvest of souls that adds numbers to the body of Christ through enrollment and baptisms. As believers grow spiritually, God gives the churches numerical increase. God sends us into the world to preach and teach the gospel with passion and conviction. The need for redemption is universal, and our task is to take this message to the world.

Attendance is an effective gauge of what's happening in a church's growth. We can read reports today from first-century churches that show how God was at work among them. Notice how naturally the Scriptures mention numbers.

So those who accepted his message were baptized,
and that day about three thousand people were added to
them (Acts 2:41).

But many of those who heard the message believed,
and the number of the men came to about five thousand (Acts 4:4).

So the preaching about God flourished, the number
of the disciples in Jerusalem multiplied greatly, and a large
group of priests became obedient to the faith (Acts 6:7).

The Lord's hand was with them, and a large number
who believed turned to the Lord (Acts 11:21).

There's nothing wrong with seeing numbers as evidence of God
at work. The danger is in seeing numbers as statistics rather than
people and in using numbers as the sole measure of growth. Statistics
have plenty of good and important uses, but by themselves they rarely
prove anything.

Numbers do indicate that the kingdom of God is increasing constantly in the world. Discounting the value of numerical growth gives
us less motivation to evangelize. In doing so, we're likely to lose sight
of the Bible's message that the window of time when people can be
saved from their sins is limited.

As the apostle Peter said, "The Lord does not delay His promise,
as some understand delay, but is patient with you, not wanting any to
perish, but all to come to repentance" (2 Pet. 3:9). God's heart is set
on reaching out to the unsaved. If we discount the value of numbers,
we risk losing touch with that heart cry from the Lord. Numerical
growth brings new life and hope into the church and reminds us to
be about our Father's business. He knows the very moment when
Christ will return to take His people to their heavenly home. With
Peter, we must conclude that this time of waiting means the Lord
wants more people to enter the kingdom.

Truly God wants more people saved. Throughout the history of the faith He has given the increase to churches that practice the five biblical functions of church growth we talked about in chapter 7. There are more than six billion people in the world today, more people alive and in need of the saving grace of God than ever before. That gives you and me the potential to reach more people than at any time in history. We live in a sea of humanity teeming with lost people whom God is working to redeem. When our work is of the Lord, we can be assured people will be saved.

Spiritual Transformation

The second result in a kingdom-focused church is spiritual transformation. If all you concentrate on is numerical growth, your growth overall will be, as my relatives back in Virginia would say, "a mile wide and half-an-inch deep." Kingdom growth isn't shallow growth. The Lord commanded us to reach out to people in His power, and He promises to redeem them. Spiritual transformation is God's work of changing a believer into the likeness of Jesus by creating a new identity in Christ and by empowering a lifelong relationship of love, trust, and obedience to glorify God.

The Bible is filled with passages comparing a new birth in Christ with childhood. This is a great analogy. People who are born again need to understand and live the true meaning of discipleship. Just as children pass a series of milestones on their way to maturity, believers go through transformational passages on their way to spiritual fulfillment. And just as children need help and encouragement to talk, walk, and develop into capable, responsible adults, new Christians need the support and guidance of the church to nurture and affirm their faith. Peter urged all believers to "grow in the grace and knowledge of our Lord and Savior Jesus Christ" (2 Pet. 3:18).

Like a group of children, disciples are in various stages of maturity. Some are babes in Christ; some are growing faster than others; some are on their way to a long and healthy life; some are stunted and undernourished. Jesus commanded us to make disciples and demonstrated by example what a disciple's life should be like. As the example of Christ is lived out in the fellowship of the church, spiritual transformation takes place.

The Scriptures frequently mention spiritual transformation. Moses' instructions should leave no doubt in anyone's mind that God's children must be taught God's Word: "Impress them on your children. Talk about them when you sit at home and when you walk along the road, when you lie down and when you get up" (Deut. 6:7 NIV).

God's gift of life through faith has two vital dimensions, both of which are highlighted in the Bible. The first is eternal life, articulated in what is perhaps the most widely known verse of all. "For God loved the world in this way: He gave His only Son, so that everyone who believes in Him will not perish but have eternal life" (John 3:16). The second dimension is the forgiveness of our sins, which comes to us the moment we believe in Christ. In that instant Christians are delivered from the guilt and penalty of their own sin and are brought into a right relationship with God. As Peter declared, "For Christ also suffered for sins once for all, the righteous for the unrighteous, that He might bring you to God, after being put to death in the fleshly realm but made alive in the spiritual realm" (1 Pet. 3:18).

These priceless gifts, eternal life and the forgiveness of sin, mark the beginning of the Christian life. After God has saved us, He longs for us to become like Him. He wants us to grow in the grace and knowledge of Jesus. Becoming a Christian is a transforming experience that radically changes us from what we were to what Christ wants us to be.

The Bible and Christian teaching give us four evidences of spiritual transformation.

1. Our Changing Relationship with Christ

Fellowship and intimacy with the Lord are essential to spiritual transformation. Growth in Christ is not only an increase in knowledge and experience but in becoming like Jesus. This relationship is the most important matter in our lives. The abundant life doesn't exist apart from Him.

Jesus doesn't invite us to be saved and then go His own way. He is eager to enter a love relationship with us, the same kind of relationship that He has with His Heavenly Father. As Jesus prayed only hours before His death, "May they all be one, just as You, Father, are in Me and I am in You. May they also be one in Us, so that the world may believe You sent Me" (John 17:21).

After Paul met Christ on the Damascus Road, he could no longer live his old life because he was a new man. He was transformed by Christ living in him. "I have been crucified with Christ," he wrote, "and I no longer live, but Christ lives in me. The life I now live in the flesh, I live by faith in the Son of God, who loved me and gave Himself for me" (Gal. 2:19–20).

2. Our Changing Relationship with Believers

The mark of a growing church is the warm, loving relationship believers enjoy among themselves. God creates each of us in His image, but we're all one of a kind, each the product of a unique set of backgrounds, cultures, ideas, opinions, and experiences. We may not agree on everything, but we are part of God's family. As different as we are, we are equal before God, and being one with Christ means we're one with one another. The Holy Spirit has many roles in our lives and in the life of the church, but none is more important than to provide unity in love.

Growing churches grow believers in a deeper relationship with Christ and other believers. When we allow Christ to live His life through us and to express Himself through what we say, think, and do, we have no trouble being in fellowship with one another. Salvation is expressed in our love for Christ and the whole family of God. Spiritual transformation draws us into a fellowship of believers that will sustain us through any trial.

As John reminds us, "Love consists in this: not that we loved God, but that He loved us and sent His Son to be the propitiation for our sins. Dear friends, if God loved us in this way, we also must love one another" (1 John 4:10–11).

3. Our Changing Relationships with Unbelievers

Jesus' followers have a passion to see unbelievers brought into a love relationship with Him. Christ promised us, "But you will receive power when the Holy Spirit has come upon you, and you will be My witnesses in Jerusalem, in all Judea and Samaria, and to the ends of the earth" (Acts 1:8).

Discipleship and evangelism are inseparable. In a real sense they are one and the same. We're called to stay in constant contact with unbelievers in order to witness to them and win them to Christ. God's plan for world redemption is to use each of us to win others to Christ. Spiritual transformation in a church results in believers' learning their responsibility to witness to the lost. People who are spiritually transformed have a deep desire to see others saved.

4. Our Changing Relationship Toward Christian Disciplines

The Christian life is built on decisions to pursue or ignore Bible reading, prayer, worship, witnessing, and faithful participation in the fellowship of believers. These activities won't produce mature Christians by themselves, but believers need to do them to grow spiritually. Growing churches nurture their members by teaching and leading them to practice Christian disciplines so that they may grow in the grace and knowledge of the Lord.

Ministry Expansion

The third result in a kingdom-focused church is ministry expansion. Young churches are busy building the foundation of their ministries with worship and open groups, which reach believers and unbelievers alike. Then, meeting a wider circle of needs in the community, these churches add Bible study and other outreach ministries. Seeing more needs, even more ministries are established. Churches learn that as they grow numerically and spiritually, the Holy Spirit opens additional ministry doors.

As churches experience the power of God working to bring the unsaved to Christ, they become more sensitive to unmet needs and expand their ministries to address them. In a kingdom-focused church, members naturally seek out new places to serve. Every believer has a gift to serve in one way or another. As Paul described it, "Now there are different gifts, but the same Spirit. . . . But one and the same Spirit is active in all these, distributing to each one as He wills" (1 Cor. 12:4, 11). As the body of Christ matures, the Holy Spirit raises up needs and opportunities for ministry as well as gifted believers to meet those needs.

The world's needs today are greater than ever. The Lord doesn't expect you to meet them in your own power. A burden like that would utterly defeat you. What God does expect, however, is that you will place your resources and abilities in His hands. He will bless them and multiply them so that you'll have more than enough to meet the needs you face. When you yield yourself and your possessions to God and follow His leadership, you can minister in His name to anyone, anywhere, anytime. Remember Jesus' words:

"Then the righteous will answer Him, 'Lord, when did we see You hungry and feed You, or thirsty and give You something to drink? When did we see You a stranger and take you in, or without clothes and clothe You? When did we see You sick, or in prison, and visit You?' And the King will answer them, 'I assure you: Whatever you did for one of the least of these brothers of Mine, you did for Me'" (Matt. 25:37–40).

God empowers us to minister according to His will with His resources. He shows us where the world needs His Word and directs us to bear the burden of love He has for the lost people there. If you think you can't do it, you need to look deeper at your faith. Remember, God is asking you to minister with His power, not your own. The Holy Spirit gifts and equips us to minister as godly stewards.

Growing churches produce stewards who expand the church's ministry. As the body grows numerically and spiritually, the Lord moves in the hearts and lives of people to do wonderful things. As the Creator of all things, God has the resources to do whatever He wants with creation through His people. As we go where He sends us, we can be assured that, in God's power, we can accomplish the work He's given us.

New ministries alone aren't a sign of a growing church. Ministries must be focused on sharing the love of Jesus with the lost. Otherwise they're no different from the hundreds of secular charitable and civic organizations. If you lose sight of your kingdom stewardship, you forfeit the power, presence, and freshness of the Holy Spirit to direct and equip you.

There may be times when the Lord leads your church to do things outside its comfort zone. Good! The more mature your congregation is as believers, the more likely God is to lead you to different—and more wonderful—ministries. In the parable of the talents, Jesus recalled how the servants' faithfulness earned them greater responsibilities. "For to everyone who has, more will be given, and he will have more than enough. But from the one who does not have, even what he has will be taken away from him" (Matt. 25:29).

A growing church will enjoy the freshness of the Lord's raising up believers to accomplish extraordinary things for the kingdom. As ministry expands, the freshness in the body of Christ reveals that the kingdom is growing.

Kingdom Advance

The fourth result, the measure of true growth in a church, is how effectively it has enlarged the kingdom. This is the Great Commission in its best and purest form, going out from local churches under the Lord's direction and protection into the mission field. Church members, gifted for ministry, serve the Lord as He directs, having moved from unbeliever, to believer, to kingdom multiplier.

Missions is the growth measure that puts every other component in its proper perspective. It is the crown of every church's ministry, proof that the people of God have embraced a biblical worldview. Jesus Christ came into the world to save every person in it, wherever they live, whatever their culture. God has one strategy for all the nations; there is one Lord, one salvation, one message to preach, and one call to repentance.

Every member of every church should be ready to preach that message and announce that call. Every believer is a minister, saved for service in the kingdom. Some will be pastors and staff, but most will minister as laymen. The roles are different, but the importance of each is equal in every way. When a church grows numerically, spiritually, and in ministry, believers become sensitive to the need to extend the gospel beyond their communities to a world lost in sin. They see the world more clearly, fields white unto harvest; and their desire to witness, win, disciple, and minister is multiplied and enlarged.

Some see opportunities within their families, churches, or neighborhoods, while others will be called to witness far from home. Wherever they go to advance the kingdom, their ministry is a natural product of the kingdom-focused church, God's perfect plan for establishing His reign on earth. Unless you go when God calls you, the lost remain eternally lost in sin and separated from God.

When Isaiah saw the Lord in His holy splendor, he confessed his sin and the sin of the people. He knew the Lord transcended anything he could ever know or experience. What Isaiah heard, however, was God calling out, "'Whom shall I send? And who will go for us?' And I said, 'Here am I. Send me!'" (Isa. 6:8 NIV).

God calls all believers with the same words. And our response to that call must be, "Here am I. Send me." You can't know the Lord's heart until you see Him as sovereign over all, longing to reach out to the unsaved. And you can't know the Lord's heart until you accept the fact that He calls you to go in His name to share the good news with a lost world. A growing church can never rest until it reaches the world for Christ, beginning with its own neighborhood and moving steadily outward under the Holy Spirit's leadership and power.

That means there's always plenty left to do. A growing church responds by sending missionaries into all the world and by praying and giving to support them. Strong missions come only from dedicated education about the importance of missions. God's people must understand that the great force behind kingdom advance in the world is missions. They also must realize that discipleship has its price: personal sacrifice and responsibility.

When a church becomes a "sending" church, gladly giving up sons and daughters, leaders and followers, pastor and staff, it is a growing church. A kingdom-focused church.

Chapter 9

Mapping Out a Strategy

M IKE IS ON A ROLL NOW. His understanding of his ministry and the nature of his church is growing. His excitement is matched only by his optimism about the future. He has a new understanding of the kingdom of God, its focus, and the nature of his church. He is ready, eager, and willing. He knows the results to expect. Nothing but success ahead, right?

Not quite, unfortunately. New insights often lead to optimism, joy, and energy. But emotion is not always transformed into effectiveness. Mike needs to remember what he has learned about the nature of the church. The key to focus and change lies within the definition.

He was on the right track with the question, If a restaurant serves food and a hotel sleeps people, what does a church do? A church is a dynamic fellowship of believers under the lordship of Christ. What it does is to make disciples, mature believers, and multiply them into kingdom ministries. When he truly understands these elements, he will be able to combine kingdom focus with the functions of a church (the why and the how), the results God desires, and then add the *what* of the church. In doing this, Mike will find a key to effectiveness and joy as a pastor like never before.

There are approximately 365,000 evangelical churches in the United States today. They come in all sizes, shapes, styles, locations, and buildings. These churches are unique in many ways, and they play a large role in shaping the lives of the believers who belong to them. In addition, they represent a powerful potential kingdom force when taken together. I use these words carefully when I say a *powerful potential force.* By some findings, nearly 35 percent of American adults claim to be born-again believers. With a population of 280 million Americans, that's 98 million Americans who claim to be Christians. Ninety-eight million! If one-third of our nation is indeed Christian, why is it that 70 percent of evangelical churches are not growing? Why do we lament the slide of morals and values and the increase in violence? Why does it feel like we're losing ground daily and our Christian influence is waning?

Let me see if I can ask it another way. What do you imagine the strategy of the average evangelical church is in respect to the lost persons who live around them? Unfortunately, the question of lost people needing Christ is generally not one churches spend a lot of time debating. The theology of salvation and the importance of the Great Commission are usually not hot topics of controversy or discussion. We know lost persons are all around us, and we know that their salvation in Christ is of utmost importance. But what, generally, is the strategy to reach them?

No Plans to Reach the Lost

If you look at the increase in U.S. population over the last twenty-five years and compare it to the decline of evangelical churches over the same period, the strategies of churches and denominations are painfully clear. There aren't any. We have no strategy to reach lost persons, no vision, and no real actions. We have seminars on church growth. We have classes on witnessing and reaching out to unbelievers, but we have few actions. We have articles in magazines, chapters in books, and denominational budgets for evangelism, but not much evangelism. In fact if you look closely, churches across America have abandoned a passion for winning the lost to Christ. We have become afraid of being offensive, fearful of coming across as insensitive, and doubtful of whether evangelism really works today.

In the face of the greatest rise of ungodliness in our nation, we have abandoned the only strategy the Bible gives us to change our world and the lives of those who live on earth today. We have cloistered ourselves in the fortresses of our buildings and adopted the approach of letting lost people remain lost while we lament the way they act and live. It's almost as if our attitude is, "We're saved and safe; let them go to hell!" I know we don't mean it that way, but our inaction speaks clearly here.

Most people who are living a life that is sending them to hell and an eternity apart from the God who loves them either don't know it or don't care. I can understand that. What I cannot understand is that many of us who are going to heaven don't care either!

We have to have a church strategy that matches the Great Commission, is built on the five biblical functions of a church, and leads to the four results we find throughout Scripture and church history. We must have a system of honoring God's will of loving those who live on earth today and evangelizing them with the truthful message of God's love for them in Christ. It is the only message that will ever make a difference in their lives.

What do we see today across our nation? Many, if not most, of our churches can be described in the shameful category mentioned above. They are unconcerned, afraid, or unwilling to evangelize. Others, thankfully, have a different and better strategy. Some leaders and churches are bravely going out week by week to evangelize lost people in their communities. They long to see people saved and in relationship to God through Christ. This is certainly a move in the right direction, but frankly it is not yet enough. The Great Commission commands us to make disciples *and* baptize them *and* teach them to observe all things He has commanded us.

The Need for a Comprehensive Model

Evangelism is the first priority of a church, but it isn't the only one. Some churches take action to get lost persons saved and baptized. Some rightly take it further and seek to assimilate believers into church membership. Others move still further in the right direction and have discipleship ministries to build the lives of believers. All of these are directionally correct, and each one is better than the previous one but is not enough.

"Wait a minute!" you say. "If any church did any of the above, it would be great, fantastic, wonderful." I agree that so few churches take these kinds of evangelism and discipleship actions that to do them would indeed be unique and fabulous. But doing all the above is still not a full biblical strategy. The Great Commission is comprehensive, and the biblical record of the early church is unmistakable in recording what must be done. It is simple, but it must be done. The New Testament model is as follows:

Make Disciples
Mature Believers
Multiply Ministries

The action plan you have for your church must include each of these important elements. To make disciples you must evangelize lost people in your community, around your area, in the nation, and across the world. We must share Christ with unbelievers any place, any time we find them. To make disciples we must lead unbelievers to Christ. Then in a local church setting, we lead them to worship, Bible study, and discipleship so they grow in the likeness of Christ. They enter a process of spiritual transformation and discover their spiritual gifts. We equip them for Christian living and for Christian ministry.

Equipped to serve the Lord, we then multiply ourselves in their lives, expanding the kingdom of God and extending our ministries. We reach the lost for Christ; we disciple and equip them to go out with us to reach others and to disciple them to go out and. . . . On and on it goes until the kingdom of God spreads around the earth and every person hears the gospel and has the opportunity to trust in Christ.

If our strategy for doing church does not include these three elements—making disciples, maturing believers, and multiplying ministries, we will never successfully build a kingdom-focused church. It would be like a professional football team focusing on its facilities, coaching staff, playbooks, and equipment but ignoring the score. The team could have the finest of a long list of characteristics and still lose every game. The object of having a football team is to win the championship and to win it every year. The object of doing church is to win the lost to Christ and, as quickly as possible, to see them mature in Christ and send them into multiplying ministries. We win or lose by what we do about *all* of the Great Commission.

I need to be clear here. God builds His kingdom through each church by working in His own time, in His own way, for His own perfect purposes—sometimes purposes we can't understand. We cannot and should not try to predict how the Lord will work to redeem people either in our neighborhood or in another community on the other side of the world.

A kingdom focus requires that God's people, individually and together, be what He wants them to be. When God demands that our lives be holy and surrendered to Him, He will not accept anything less. We aren't required to be perfect because God knows that's impossible. But we are required to be dedicated, obedient, and set apart to Him.

When we confess our sin, we receive immediate forgiveness and are restored to a right relationship with God. With our repentance and His forgiveness, we have everything we need to grow spiritually, evangelize the world, minister, and disciple believers. We walk in fellowship with the Lord. At that point we can turn our attention to the lost.

Lost people may or may not have any interest in religion. They may or may not be on a church roll. Drifting in sin and separated from God, they might live next door to you, work at the desk next to you, or be someone far away. They know nothing of God's love, grace, forgiveness, or eternal life.

They are the bull's-eye in the target of the kingdom-focused church.

Because kingdom-focused churches share certain key characteristics, they also share specific ways of putting those characteristics into practice. Now don't worry, I'm not about to launch off into Ten Steps to a Kingdom-Focused Church. As I've said before, that kind of approach puts the spotlight on procedures instead of on results, and that's not what this book is about. However, there are particular tools that make the road to a kingdom focus straighter than it would be without them and make the trip a lot less frustrating and stressful. They are every church's road map to success.

Grounded in Biblical Principles

A church has to respond effectively to the needs and concerns of the neighborhood where God has placed it, and to do that it must be solidly grounded in biblical principles. The world looks to the church for answers to basic and deeply felt questions like: Why do we exist? What are we supposed to do with our lives? What difference does God make in my life?

Many believers and nonbelievers alike are unaware of the kingdom of God. They have trouble seeing God at work around them. They have no confidence in Christ and live for themselves alone. They don't know how to pray, follow God's commands, support the church in its work, or live triumphantly in a fallen world.

Through the Scriptures we teach men and women to seek God's kingdom above all else and to pursue an intimate relationship with the Father that produces Christlikeness. The Bible shows them how to understand and live in a fallen, sinful, and unfair world. Through the Word church members and visitors see God at work and join Him, adjusting their view of the world to embrace a biblical view.

Only in the Bible can they see the full scope and power of the Great Commission, claiming the promise of salvation for themselves and then taking that good news away with them to share with others. Without the driving force of the Great Commission, the growth of any church congregation is little more than a misguided attempt to inflate its membership numbers, try out new marketing techniques, or try something different.

The Great Commission isn't just biblical history, nor is it a mandate given only to a select few. It is the defining contemporary command to followers of Jesus in any era. Believers on a mission for Christ through His church are joy-filled Christians who find a richness and assurance in life that comes only from the Holy Spirit. The Great Commission is the driving force of any church strategy. The elements of making, maturing, and multiplying disciples are clearly seen within it, and it serves as the starting point of doing church right.

Looking at the Church's Culture

The next step in a successful strategy to build a kingdom-focused church is to understand and view a church's culture. The culture is the local context of a church's life that shapes the way it views itself and leads to its unique style and identity. Understanding your church's culture is important in developing a successful strategy because it frees your church to be and become what God wants it to be. No two churches are alike, nor should they be. Your church should not copy another's success or models unless they fit what the Lord is doing in your congregation.

Examining your culture helps you wrestle with two important strategic questions, who are we today, and what do we think the Lord wants us to become? The answers to these two questions are vital. Every church is different, and each has a different culture, history, and experience. Your church's culture explains why you do church today as you do. Your style, history, traditions, and methods have roots in the past, which affect the present. Your culture also reflects your church's image and personality in your community. This is a powerful influence that may help attract people or may turn them away. In effect, it becomes one key factor that people will use to determine if your church is the right fit for them.

A church's culture is characterized by the interaction of four forces:

1. The leadership styles of the pastor, key staff, and lay leaders
2. The demographic characteristics of the people and the community
3. The current life cycle of the church (growing, stable, or declining)
4. The current life cycle of the community (growing, stable, or declining)

When a church culture fails to reflect the context of its community, it has difficulty finding a kingdom focus. If significant generational differences exist, then similar problems occur. A kingdom-focused strategy must take the church's culture into account, or effectiveness in ministry becomes impossible.

Can you see how a kingdom-focused church strategy is beginning to unfold? You first build your strategy on the driving force of the Great Commission. Next, you look at your church to identify its history, tradition, and culture. Then, compare what you find inside your church to what you face on the outside. Finally, address how you will overcome significant differences.

Look Where God Is Leading

Finally you take a look at where God will lead you in the future. Sometimes this means creating a compelling image of an achievable future. But be careful; no person alive can anticipate what the Lord will do in and through your church in the future. We do not create the future. God does, and He is the only One who knows what it looks like.

If you pour everything we've talked about so far in this chapter into the kingdom-focus funnel, you begin to refine and distill all this talk into action. If you're still with me here, you know that to be a successful church you have to have a kingdom focus. Everything you do has to lift up and strengthen evangelism in some way or another. You know the characteristics of a kingdom-focused church and how the quality and intensity of that focus can be measured.

Now we have the building blocks of a great kingdom-focused church strategy. The five functions of the church will give you a ministry infrastructure, and the four results will allow you to measure your progress. If you're not seeing kingdom results, then the problem is either a lack of Great Commission focus or a failure to carry out one or more of the five functions.

With this in mind, let's turn to the part of the process that is going to give you the results you have desired and prayed for throughout your ministry. It's time to put the kingdom-focused church concepts into practice. Church practice comes directly from the intentional strategy that you determined God is leading you to follow. Church practice is balancing the essential actions you'll use to engage your people in the five biblical functions of evangelism, discipleship, fellowship, ministry, and worship.

The five functions were introduced in the previous chapter. Also, you may have read them in my book *Kingdom Principles for Church Growth*[1] or Rick Warren's *The Purpose-Driven Church*.[2] There's no limit to the number of articles, tapes, and books on the functions and purposes of a local church. However, the reality is that unless you implement them together and fully, you can never have a true kingdom-focused church. It will never happen. No matter how successful you may be in one area of church life, the other areas will suffer or fail to develop, and one day it all catches up. You may have terrific growth, but if you fail to mature the disciples you make, you will have trouble soon. If you focus on fellowship and worship and overlook evangelism and ministry, you will plateau numerically and spiritually after a while.

You need to consider carefully questions like these: What do we think the Lord wants us to be, do, and accomplish? What kind of church do we really intend to be and to become? And what is the most efficient and effective way to reach people for Christ, mature them, and put them into our multiplying ministries?

Everyone realizes that for many churches strategy is often not intentional or worse, is nonexistent. A local church strategy describes a clear and deliberate set of intentions that, when woven together as a whole, drive every decision that determines what a local church does. A comprehensive strategy helps give a vision to the work of a church, and it helps in decision making, that is, decisions that determine what is and is not going to be done. But strategy must be put into practice, and practice must come from a biblical model.

To apply an institutional or business model in a church is disastrous. A biblical vision added to a biblical strategy coupled with a biblical model is powerful and successful.

Stay with me here. Don't panic and give up on what God is teaching you right now. If you have never thought of these things or successfully put them into practice, don't worry. Most church leaders haven't either. If you are like me, you've never been trained or seen something modeled like this.

Remember the illustration of the young man driving the race car at the Indy 500? Most of us have had training and experience to do many great and important things. We may preach, teach, and care for people with great joy and ease. But to change the culture of our churches is another matter altogether. We are trained to maintain and grow successful churches but not broken-down, declining ones. Well, as we have already seen, most evangelical churches are undergoing enormous change, and growth isn't the primary result.

Churches do not have to die, pastors do not have to fail in their leadership, and believers do not have to remain dormant throughout their lives. Let's remember that the Lord wants us to know Him fully, serve Him fully, and accomplish His purposes fully. *He wants us to succeed!* He gave us the Bible and the Holy Spirit to direct us to a kingdom focus. Your leadership is actually under the will of God and the direction of the Holy Spirit. The Holy Spirit shows us the answers to the questions we asked above concerning strategy. He is your guide, resource, and power to do what the Lord wants you and your church to do.

A Model from the Life of Jesus

I am going to show you a model and process for ministry which will give you a clear understanding of how to get the will of God into a successful strategy, then show you how to get that strategy into practice. It is just a matter of seeing what to do and how to correlate the work of the functions into one consistent, simple, effective system. Let's take a minute to see how this is so clearly illustrated in Jesus' own earthly ministry.

Matthew 9 records a busy day in the life of our Lord. Jesus spent the day forgiving a paralytic man of his sins and giving him strength to walk (vv. 1–8). He commanded Matthew to follow Him as a disciple (v. 9). He had an altercation with the Pharisees over eating with sinners and tax collectors (vv. 10–13). He healed a woman who touched His robe on His way to raise a little girl from the dead (vv. 18–26). He went on to heal two blind men (vv. 27–31). And then He drove a demon from a man who was brought to Him (vv. 32–34). After a draining day, Jesus continued into many other villages and towns ministering. In verses 35–38 we see Jesus' heart for a kingdom-focused church ministry.

> Then Jesus went to all the towns and villages, teaching in their synagogues, preaching the good news of the kingdom, and healing every disease and every sickness. When He saw the crowds, He felt compassion for them, because they were weary and worn out, like sheep without a shepherd. Then He said to His disciples, "The harvest is abundant, but the workers are few. Therefore, pray to the Lord of the harvest to send out workers into His harvest."

A closer look at this passage reveals the balanced model of ministry Jesus used. His model cannot be improved upon and is essential to us in church ministry today. His model includes four basic strategies that you'll encounter over and over again in the Gospels as well as the rest of the New Testament. Let's look at each phrase carefully.

"Then Jesus went to all the towns and villages, teaching in their synagogues, preaching the good news of the kingdom, and healing every disease and every sickness" (Matt. 9:35). We see here that He used corporate worship to help believers celebrate God's grace and mercy. He also used corporate worship to proclaim God's truth and to evangelize the lost in a dynamic atmosphere of encountering the presence, holiness, and revelation of God Almighty. Corporate worship is where believers and unbelievers come together. All the biblical functions of the church are present in a worship service, and the Great Commission is fulfilled.

"When He saw the crowds, He felt compassion for them, because they were weary and worn out, like sheep without a shepherd" (Matt. 9:36). Moving from the large worship assembly of the synagogue, He moved to groups of individuals to meet their needs. The groups were open, meaning all were invited. Open groups exist to lead people to faith in Christ and to build believers by engaging them in evangelism, discipleship, fellowship, ministry, and worship. He mixed the hurting and spiritually ignorant with His disciples and taught, preached, ministered, and welcomed anyone to hear the good news that God loved them.

"Then He said to His disciples, 'The harvest is abundant, but the workers are few'" (Matt. 9:37). Jesus left the crowds and gathered the disciples in a closed group. Closed groups exist to build kingdom leaders and to equip believers to serve the Lord. The Lord was training His followers and moving them toward spiritual transformation.

"Therefore, pray to the Lord of the harvest to send out workers into His harvest" (Matt. 9:38). Jesus revealed that the true purpose of the training was to send out teams of the disciples to preach the good news of the kingdom of God and to train new disciples for ministry—to go back into the harvest fields filled with others ready to receive Christ as Lord.

A Kingdom-Focused Church Model and Process

Jesus' goal was to multiply Himself in and through others. His pattern and model?

1. Corporate Worship
2. Open Groups
3. Closed Groups
4. Ministry Teams

Corporate worship, open groups, and ministry teams serve as entry points into the church for unbelievers. When they are saved, they are brought into the fellowship of believers. Mixing with members, new believers come into the body of Christ and begin the journey of following Christ.

A Kingdom-Focused Church Model and Process

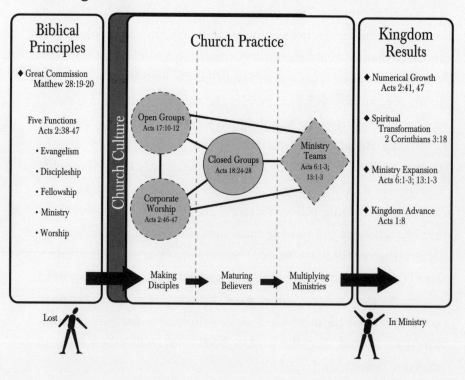

Closed groups are used to mature believers in Christ and to help them discover their gifts for ministry. As they mature, believers are moved into multiplying ministries.

Looking at the model and process diagram on the previous page, you can see the entire process. Unbelievers are outside of corporate worship and open groups. The church evangelizes them and brings them to the experience of worship and small-group Bible study. When they become Christians, they are given discipleship opportunities in order to mature and be prepared for ministry.

Let's review the multiplying process in its three stages.

Making Disciples:
- Evangelizing unbelievers
- Experiencing fellowship, worship, and Bible study with other believers
- Beginning assimilation into the church

Maturing Believers:
- Being spiritually transformed
- Equipping for ministry
- Developing accountability
- Learning to be a leader

Multiplying Ministries:
- Participating in ministry through service in the church
- Participating in missions outside the church
- Reproducing themselves in and through others

The successful pathway to a kingdom-focused church leads through a series of experiences that turn a new believer into a new voice for the kingdom. New disciples are welcomed into corporate worship and into smaller groups that combine new Christians, mature Christians, and unbelievers. Maturing believers then move into more intense, deeper study in the company of other believers who are developing their leadership skills and accountability. In the multiplying stage, Christians focus on ministry within and missions outside the church. This is a *kingdom* focus.

What are the kingdom results you can expect as you follow this church model and process? Jesus pointed us in this direction when He said:

> "I assure you: The Son is not able to do anything on His own, but only what He sees the Father doing. For whatever the Father does, these things the Son also does in the same way. For the Father loves the Son and shows Him everything He is doing, and He will show Him greater works than these so that you will be amazed" (John 5:19–20).

> "I assure you: The one who believes in Me will also do the works that I do. And he will do even greater works than these, because I am going to the Father" (John 14:12).

Chapter 10

MAKING DISCIPLES: CORPORATE WORSHIP

I︎T IS SUNDAY MORNING and the service is in progress as Mike looks across the congregation. It is the fourth Sunday of the new format, and what he sees is not pretty. As the worship team sings its fifth new song and the people stare at the new projection screen, he notices that a few older folks start to sit. He glances at his watch, noting everyone has been standing for twelve minutes. He looks again and is disappointed to find the congregation is no longer singing with the praise team. Mike realizes that something is at work here that is greater than change or custom, something that is striking at the very heart of worship. "What is worship, anyway?" he asks. Once again Mike has stumbled onto the right question. Whatever a church does must have a kingdom focus and a biblical warrant while it makes, matures, and multiplies disciples.

It's time to put everything together. Remember, a kingdom-focused strategy is simply taking biblical principles and putting them together for effective ministry. The Great Commission keeps us focused; the five functions define our work; the four results are the outcomes we're looking for; and the model and process (MAP) is the way to put it all together.

We begin with the entry point of a disciple's journey from our perspective. Lost people have little or no church perspective. Generally, they are not looking for anything from the church as it might affect them. They may have opinions about churches or even expectations of what they do (such as charitable work, weddings, funerals, and so forth), but most unbelievers have no notion of how they might fit into a church's structure and programming.

We, however, must have a clear view of what we are and what we are doing. The MAP is a great help here. Unless we know what to do and how to do it, then our actions tend to be disconnected or fragmented. Perhaps the worst thing that happens is for a church to have success in one area because it hides problems in other areas. For instance, if a church has a large worship service that grows exponentially but fails in discipleship, then people who come are left undiscipled and are not transformed. Rootless, they are easy targets for doctrinal confusion, inappropriate behavior, discouragement, and burnout.

The MAP, however, shows us how to understand the "what" of a church and apply the "how" of a church successfully. Using this simple tool, we can analyze our church and its ministries.

The first circle we examine in the MAP represents corporate worship. Of course, worship is something only believers can do, but unbelievers can attend services and watch believers worship. In fact, worship is one of the greatest tools of evangelism a church possesses. If we remember what we learned from Jesus' strategy in Matthew 9, we realize that worship is not just an emotional experience where believers and unbelievers come together. A kingdom-focused church uses worship as a key part of its strategy.

Corporate worship exists for believers to celebrate God's grace and mercy, to proclaim God's truth, and evangelize the lost in an atmosphere of encountering the presence, holiness, and revelation of Almighty God.

A Kingdom-Focused Church Model and Process

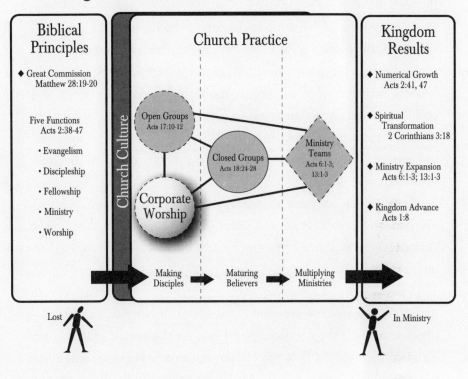

Worship that transforms is the response of believers to the presence, holiness, and revelation of Almighty God. This powerful act is an effective tool in disciple making. Those who are unbelievers come and observe or experience what believers do in worship. When worship is right, it is as if the kingdom of God comes in a spiritual presence and reality that is unlike anything else on earth. Spirit-filled worship is powerful and effective in leading people to Christ.

Transforming worship that reaches unbelievers and transforms believers must be led by worship leaders who have a kingdom focus, a Great Commission mind-set, and a passion for the living God. They must understand the cultural context of those they lead—both believers and unbelievers—and they must themselves be transformed through the worship experience.

Sunday morning worship is the top of the funnel. The "in box." It's where the journey from unbeliever to Christian to kingdom multiplier begins, the point of entry for most people who eventually become members of your congregation. To build membership and build the kingdom, a church has to get worship right. The service has to be a transforming experience for believers. It also has to welcome unbelievers into the fellowship and encourage them to become involved.

The worship service is a place where believers and unbelievers can mingle comfortably. From the committed Christian to the merely curious, everybody is made to feel a part of the people assembled to praise God.

I have a tape of a worship service that I listen to periodically. It never fails to move me emotionally as I hear the singing and preaching. I remember the occasion, and I can see the people's faces as we gathered together on that hot Sunday morning. There is something different about the tape, however. I can't understand a word anyone is saying! It is a recording of a worship service in Kenya, Africa, I participated in nearly twenty years ago. The Kenyans are singing praises to the Lord, all the preachers but me speak in their tribal dialect, and the prayers are unintelligible to me. But wow! What a worship service!

Worship styles are as varied as the cultures and people that embrace them. The fact that we worship is more important than how we do it. The form of our praise, which changes, is a distant second to the purpose, which doesn't. That purpose is encountering God in worship and being changed by His presence.

Elements of Worship

God is the object and subject of all proper worship, but you can't forget that people are there because they're looking for something. Meeting people's spiritual and emotional needs should be the people-centered intent of every worship service. And whether your service is traditional or contemporary, the Bible prescribes eight elements of worship. I'm not telling you what to do here, but I am pointing out that all eight were practiced by the early church, and all eight are characteristic of successful kingdom-focused churches.

1. Prayer

Prayer is communicating with God in a way that makes you aware of His presence. Jesus urged His followers not to pray like hypocrites, showing off for everyone, but to pray in secret, without vain repetition, and to pray for God's kingdom to come. Through the example of the Model Prayer, He also told them to pray for daily bread, deliverance from temptation, forgiveness, deliverance from evil, and to revere God in all His power and glory. During the Sermon on the Mount Jesus reminded His listeners, "But seek first the kingdom of God and His righteousness, and all these things will be provided for you" (Matt. 6:33).

Prayer was a central component of worship in the early churches. Paul encouraged Christ's followers to pray for anyone in need. He told them to pray for the spread of the gospel too, and for sinners. To the Thessalonians He said, "Pray constantly. Give thanks in everything, for this is God's will for you in Christ Jesus" (1 Thess. 5:17–18).

2. Praise

Praise expresses adoration and thanks to God for His character, being, and work. It helps the congregation understand the reality of God's kingdom and His reign over the world in their lives. Praise was a major element in the early churches' worship experience. God's people often sang songs and hymns of praise. Throughout the Old Testament the Israelites praised God in songs for their deliverance, for His miracles, and for His intervention in their lives. Early believers praised Jesus in songs for what He had done for them.

Quoting Old Testament prophecy, Paul reminded the believers in Rome:

As it is written:

Therefore I will praise You among the Gentiles,

and I will sing psalms to Your name.

Again it says: "Rejoice, you Gentiles, with His

people!" And again:

Praise the Lord, all you Gentiles;

all the peoples should praise Him! (Rom. 15:9–11).

Praise is a major element of worship in the kingdom-focused church. The people praise the Lord for creating them and for redeeming them in Christ. God's praise isn't just an emotional outburst from the heart. Christians come before the Lord to praise Him because He has told them to do so. Our praise is not because He has blessed us and done good things for us, and so we think it's only fair to reciprocate. We praise Him because He wants and commands us to and because He alone is worthy of praise.

Praise, then, isn't driven by feelings but by obedience. The only surefire ticket to a boring service is if the focus is on ourselves and our church rather than on God.

3. Confession and Repentance

God restores fellowship when people acknowledge that their sin is real and repent by turning from their sin to God. Confession is at the heart of worship. You can't just come along for the ride. You can't listen passively to music, prayers, and sermons and not be affected and changed by them. People of the congregation are there to have their minds, hearts, and lives changed and to dedicate themselves to God.

After we experience worship, we're never the same. We see our sins and shortcomings in stark relief, cry out in confession, and rejoice that the Lord will forgive and heal us. God assures us, "If my people, who are called by my name, will humble themselves and pray and seek my face and turn from their wicked ways, then will I hear from heaven and will forgive their sin and will heal their land" (2 Chron. 7:14 NIV).

4. Profession of Faith

Profession of faith in the Father, Son, and Holy Spirit gives worshipers the opportunity to acknowledge and respond to God's Word and work. By confessing our faith in the Holy Trinity, we declare that God alone is our Creator, Redeemer, and Sustainer, and that He alone is worthy of our glory, honor, and praise.

As Paul wrote to the believers in Rome, "If you confess with your mouth, 'Jesus is Lord,' and believe in your heart that God raised Him from the dead, you will be saved. With the heart one believes, resulting in righteousness, and with the mouth one confesses, resulting in salvation" (Rom. 10:9–10).

5. Scripture Reading and Study

God transforms the church through his Word. Hearing, reading, and studying Scripture are essential to a healthy Christian life. It's through the Scriptures that the Holy Spirit draws our attention to God and to our fellowship with Him.

After His resurrection Jesus appeared to two of the disciples on the road to Emmaus who had no idea they were talking with the risen Lord. When Jesus asked them why they looked so sad, they told Him about the crucifixion and burial of Christ and admitted their doubts that He would actually rise from the dead. Jesus reproved them for their unbelief and held up the Scriptures as proof of what would happen. "Then beginning with Moses and all the Prophets, He interpreted for them in all the Scriptures the things concerning Himself" (Luke 24:27).

The response of the two followers should encourage us all: "Weren't our hearts ablaze within us while He was talking with us on the road and explaining the Scriptures to us?" (Luke 24:32).

In Jerusalem Jesus demonstrated His return from the dead by showing the disciples His pierced hands and feet. "Then He told them, 'These are My words that I spoke to you while I was still with you, that everything written about Me in the Law of Moses, the Prophets, and the Psalms must be fulfilled.' Then He opened their minds to understand the Scriptures" (Luke 24:44–45).

The Word of God was precious and essential to the people of the early church. It's no less precious and essential to the church today.

6. Preaching

God uses the preaching of the Word to teach, challenge, confront, convict, and exhort His congregation to obey. Preaching is central in worship services because it focuses on the Lord. It's the church's responsibility to proclaim His Word and His truth everywhere.

Nothing can substitute for preaching, which speaks God's truth to His people and prepares them to be His messengers.

When we worship God, we come before Him in prayer, confession, and praise to hear the preaching of the Word.

What you have heard from me in the presence of
many witnesses, commit to faithful men who will be
able to teach others also (2 Tim. 2:2).

7. The Lord's Supper and Baptism

Jesus established the ordinances of the Lord's Supper and baptism as dramatic and memorable symbols to make the congregation aware of His work on their behalf. They are two beautiful, moving acts of worship Jesus gave us to remember Him.

Imagine what it was like in the upper room in those moments when Jesus passed the broken bread among His disciples hours before His crucifixion, saying, "Do this in remembrance of Me" (Luke 22:19). Then the men shared the cup, "the new covenant" in Jesus' blood shed for all sinners.

Earlier John the Baptist had been surprised that Jesus wanted to be baptized. Yet Jesus insisted it was appropriate in order to "fulfill all righteousness."

After Jesus was baptized, He went up immediately
from the water. The heavens suddenly opened for Him,
and He saw the Spirit of God descending like a dove
and coming down on Him. And there came a voice
from heaven:
This is My beloved Son.
I take delight in Him! (Matt. 3:16–17).

Christians are to follow Jesus' example by making baptism a foundational element of their worship. On the day of Pentecost, everyone who heard Peter's message asked him and the other apostles what they should do. Peter answered that they should repent and be baptized "in the name of Jesus the Messiah for the forgiveness of your sins, and you will receive the gift of the Holy Spirit" (Acts 2:38). These two ordinances, baptism and the Lord's Supper, are vital elements of genuine worship.

8. Offerings

A Christian's giving of self, abilities, tithes, and offerings are responses of obedient stewardship, gratitude, and trust. To worship fully means to give yourself in obedience to God.

First and above all, our lives are an offering to the Lord. Paul described giving of ourselves in Romans 12:1. "I urge you to present your bodies as a living sacrifice, holy and pleasing to God; this is your spiritual worship." We should also give of our means because giving is an act of worship and a recognition of His lordship over our lives.

In his final instructions to the church at Philippi, Paul gave thanks for their generosity.

"And you, Philippians, know that in the early days
of the gospel, when I left Macedonia, no church shared
with me in the matter of giving and receiving except
you alone. For even in Thessalonica you sent gifts for
my need several times. Not that I seek the gift, but
I seek the fruit that is increasing to your account. . . .
And my God will supply all your needs according to
His riches in glory in Christ Jesus" (Phil. 4:15–17, 19).

The Focus of Worship

The pastor is the leader of worship and must always take this responsibility seriously. No matter if he uses a worship team, a worship leader, or if he plans all or little of the actual service itself, he's still the leader. And he *must* carefully plan worship.

I have reached a point in my life where my eyes are doing strange things. I have been nearsighted for most of my life, but that is just one of my problems. About five years ago I began to notice that my arms were not long enough for me to read effectively. Then to make matters worse, my doctor told me that I would soon need help in the area between where I read and where I see far away. In short, I need help focusing my sight on several different levels.

Worship is really no different. We need to focus first and foremost on God. God is the only One who needs to be worshiped and satisfied with our worship. Worship must focus on the Lord alone and *never, but never* on any other person, believer or unbeliever. I truly believe that only Christians can worship God. The Bible expressly states that the only person who can worship the Lord is the one who can worship in spirit and truth (John 4:24).

The second focus of worship should be believers, in order to help them celebrate the presence and advance of the kingdom of God in the world. Believers can be wonderfully transformed in worship, and we should do all that we can as worship leaders to see that they are.

Finally, however, we can focus on unbelievers who can see and feel the true worship of the one and only God. We can focus on them and make it easy and inviting for them to come to Christ. Let's remember that we are defining corporate worship as a strategy to reach people who are not Christians. There is much we can say about worship in the life of a believer that is important and that we need to understand, but our aim here is using worship as a strategy to make disciples. Too few churches have a disciple-making worship strategy.

"What about style?" you ask. You have to use the style that meets the needs of the believers in your church and the unbelievers you seek to reach. *Style* is not the issue; *strategy* is. And it helps to keep things in balance if you keep believers and unbelievers in focus. If you are in a church that has one style of worship that you think does not fit those you seek to reach, be careful about how much change you introduce into your service. Do it, but do it slowly and with a clearly communicated strategy. If you have to, start another service at a different time or even on a different day. Focus on the Lord first, and make sure you never do anything that would dishonor Him. After that, use any style you need in order to reach people for Christ.

The church is responsible for reaching unbelievers for Christ. Remember that a kingdom-focused church will naturally integrate believers and unbelievers in worship.

Chapter 11

MAKING DISCIPLES: OPEN GROUPS

M IKE TAKES THE FOLDER LABELED "SMALL GROUPS" out of the file drawer and opens it. He finds his notes from the last four conferences he attended and spreads them out on the worktable. "So many options, but which is best for us?" he asks. He looks at the brochures attached to his notes. The Chicago seeker-driven conference, the West Coast purpose-driven conference, the Houston cell-church conference, and the state Sunday School training and leadership conference are all laid before him.

"I can't exactly draw the correct one out of a bowl, so what should I do?" he muses. "I know. I'll start with what we need and how much time we have. Something like this," he goes on. "What groups will help us *make, mature,* and *multiply* the greatest number of people?"

Bingo! Our young pastor has just moved far and fast toward becoming an effective pastor and church leader. The choice of a small-group ministry should be based on the kingdom focus of the church.

What Pastor Mike needs is a way to involve his people in the greatest opportunity for the church to make disciples, mature them, and equip them for a ministry that multiplies the effectiveness of his church and realizes the greatest kingdom results. Open groups are important because they are person-centered, lay-led, and Bible-based.

Open groups exist to lead people to faith in the Lord Jesus Christ and to transform them into Christlikeness by engaging them in evangelism, discipleship, fellowship, ministry, and worship. Open groups are small kingdom communities designed to bring believers and unbelievers together in an atmosphere of compassion to share the gospel.

Person-Centered

Effective open groups are never content-centered, although content is important. Too often pastors and church leaders focus on the

A Kingdom-Focused Church Model and Process

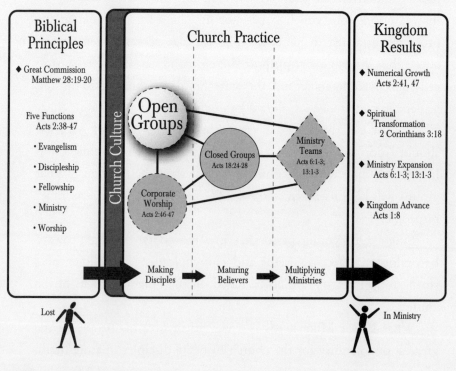

content of small groups and fail to take into account the reason they exist. Small groups are a kingdom tool for reaching persons for Christ and bringing them into a transforming relationship with Him. They must focus on the person first and foremost.

I have observed many church curriculum guides outlining the courses and studies offered to prospective participants. Some are well conceived and put together with attractive brochures. In the end, however, they do not take into consideration the needs of the persons who will come. Your small groups must focus on the needs of the persons you reach and train. What do they need at this time of life? What skills or understanding would help them to live for Christ or be spiritually transformed?

Every individual is on a life path in his or her relationship to Christ. Those who do not know Him must be reached. Those who do must be discipled and trained in kingdom ministry. Your small groups must focus on the spiritual life needs of your people.

Lay-Led

Recently I visited in a large church whose pastor had just left in frustration and confusion. The church was reeling under the shock and embarrassment of his departure. When I visited with the leaders, they had only one criticism of this man they loved and respected. By consensus they told me, "He wouldn't let us minister." Probing deeper, I realized that the pastor and staff directed all ministry and never really allowed the people an opportunity to exercise their spiritual gifts.

Pastor, open groups are a kingdom gift to you. They are powerful tools for building kingdom-focused churches, but you must understand that they are successful only when laypersons lead them. You must guide your leaders to understand what your small groups can do, but they must lead! Do not do their ministry for them. Allow them to be used by God to accomplish His will in these groups. In this way you can multiply yourself one hundred times more than if you try to do these things yourself.

God has raised you up to lead your people and to multiply yourself in them. Small groups are one of your best tools to do this.

Bible-Based

Today there are as many resources for small groups as there are small groups. Everything from Bible studies to arts and crafts classes. If you want to build a kingdom-focused church, however, the Bible must be the centerpiece for all your small groups do. Why, you ask? For several reasons.

First, only the Bible can meet the true spiritual needs of your people anytime and all the time. Anything else is just opinion, and one opinion is as good as another. The Bible is God's written revelation of Himself to us. There is no substitute, and we only hurt ourselves when we depart from it.

Another reason is that the Bible is a living document which, as a resource, is able to meet the needs of every person who comes to a small group. No other resource can claim to be alive and able to do what the Bible does.

Finally, Scripture reveals the disciple's needs and God's answer. It is not conjecture or opinion when the Word speaks to us, nor is it a suggestion when God provides an answer. The Bible is the Holy Spirit's tool to convict us of sin and to build us up into Christ.

A Strategy for Open Groups

It is one thing to know the theory behind open groups but quite another to develop an effective strategy for them. What follows is a tried, tested, and proven strategy for maximizing your open groups. Remember, they are person-centered, lay-led, and Bible-based. Like worship, open groups are also the place where believers and unbelievers come together. Every open group has a focus on two kinds of people. For the sake of clarity, I want to call them *prospects* and *pupils*.

Prospects

Whether you do small groups in Sunday School, cell groups, affinity groups, or home Bible fellowships, you have to focus on prospects or pupils. Prospects come in three categories and must be approached a bit differently.

1. Prospects who are not believers. These are the individuals your church has discovered in various ways who have been identified as lost, unsaved, or outside the kingdom of God. No matter what else we do for them, such as inviting them to special church events, worship services, or other activities, the focus must be evangelizing them and leading them to Christ. Lost persons are our responsibility, and we cannot leave them alone to die in their sins. Unbelievers are to be evangelized as a part of our open-group strategy. The easiest evangelism in the kingdom is in open groups. Lost people come under the influence of believers as they experience love, ministry, and witness. It is much easier to evangelize a person in a group than in any other context.

2. Prospects who are believers but are not in church. There are thousands, if not millions, of people around the world who are believers but have not found a church. They may have just moved into the community or may have lived there for years but for some reason are not involved in ministry anywhere. It is spiritually unhealthy, if not dangerous, for a believer to be unattached to a local church. Believers in relationship to one another are the heart and soul of a kingdom-focused church. Any believer who is unchurched is not in God's will.

There is much talk today about the body of Christ. This is generally done in a vague, nondescript manner. The Old Testament speaks often about the people of God, and the New Testament speaks about the body of Christ. But the body of Christ is nothing without members belonging to one another, loving one another, worshiping with one another, and building one another up in Christ. In the New Testament, most of the references to church refer to a local assembly of believers who exist for kingdom purposes. Believers who are not in church must be reached and brought into a local body. This is not so much a plea for formal membership as it is a plea for them to obey God's will. Believers need to be in a local church and in small groups of believers in order to minister, fellowship, witness, worship, and learn. When you identify unchurched believers, go after them and enlist them in your open groups.

3. Prospects who are believers and in your local church but not in small groups should be reached in order to enlist them in effective ministry. The church at worship becomes the church at work in open groups. Today most churches have many members who come to worship services and enjoy the music, preaching, and excitement. But a member does not minister or expand the kingdom in a worship service. Open groups allow the five biblical functions to be done effectively, allowing every member to find an opportunity for ministry.

Open groups are foundational to a believer's continuing transformation into Christlikeness and effective kingdom impact. This simply cannot be done in worship by itself. The most effective strategy for reaching *prospects,* then, is evangelizing unbelievers, enlisting unchurched believers, and enrolling church members not now in open groups.

Pupils

Once enrolled, prospects become pupils. These believers are then engaged in a Bible-based curriculum, which focuses on their life needs and begins a foundational ministry for their transformation. Participation is ongoing for believers in open groups because, as we shall see, they are the foundational strategy for all that a church does.

Open groups fulfill the Great Commission by evangelizing the lost, discipling believers through Bible study, providing fellowship by building relationships with believers and unbelievers, engaging them in ministry to and with fellow class members. Open groups form a powerful alliance with worship services (large open groups) to build the kingdom of God effectively.

It is perhaps a misnomer to call an open group a "class." They are classes in the sense that the Bible is studied, but they are much more. They are kingdom entities built on the five functions of the church. They are living organisms built for the people who attend.

Multiplying for Kingdom Effectiveness

If you want to grow a church, you must either start something new, like new ministries or worship services, or multiply what you currently do. There is no way to grow a healthy church without starting something new. Companies use this simple principle every day as they build new stores in new locations or buy existing businesses. To expand they must do something more than what they are presently doing.

How will you grow your church? When you fill up the worship center, will you have built up your people? Will you be able to mature your worshipers and multiply yourself in and through their lives? The fastest way to build a kingdom-focused church is by multiplying open groups. You can increase the number who come to worship, you can add ministries, and you can erect buildings, but nothing builds the kingdom faster than open groups. They are dynamite compared to other alternatives.

Open groups are truly a gift from God to reach unbelievers and extend the kingdom of God. The simplest strategy (and the most effective ever designed) has five basic principles.[1] No matter where you are, no matter what your church's size, and no matter what you have tried before, these principles work. In other resources and conferences, this is where the presenter says to you, "Don't try this when you get back home." But this is where I say to you, "Do exactly what I say, and I guarantee you great results!" Let's look at the principles (that were developed by a layman, by the way).

1. Identify the Prospects

Do you remember the three categories of prospects we listed above? Well, you can't reach categories, can you? No, you have to identify people. That's right, by name, address, telephone number, or relationship to someone in your church. How many people would you say you could identify right now as prospects for any of your open groups?

The theory of open groups is exciting. There are thousands of books on Sunday School, cell groups, fellowship groups, and affinity groups. I love to read about the various theories and philosophies. I always get excited when someone talks about the successes of Sunday School classes or other small groups. But no strategy or philosophy can take the place of identifying those individuals and families we seek to reach. Passion and purpose must be given to real people with real names and jobs and addresses and families.

I suggest that right now you begin to identify those who *could* come to your open groups if they *would*. Don't worry right now if they will or not. Just identify them and put their names on a list for future reference.

2. Develop an Organization

A second key to an open-group strategy is the development of an organization to handle the growth that God will give once you start to reach prospects and teach pupils. Most of us wait until the last minute to develop organizations we need. But if you are going to have a kingdom-focused church, it is essential to think about your organization before you begin. If you don't, then you will likely experience rapid growth only to lose what you've gained when the people you reach somehow get lost in the shuffle of where to go and how to be served.

Organization does not make you successful, but the lack of organization will lead you to failure. You need to consider what kinds of open groups you are going to have and what kind of structure they will need. Remember, these groups are lay-led, so you have to give structure to the leaders if they are to be effective. Don't let your strategy be dictated by your current or future organization. Rather, let your strategy *dictate* your organization. If you have Sunday School groups for children, youth, and adults, then you have to have an organization to allow these groups to succeed. If you have home groups, affinity groups, or cells, then you will have a structure unique to them.

An organization is a formal arrangement of people assigned to specific tasks that implement your chosen strategy. Someone has to be responsible for all of an organization's work, and others have to be accountable for parts of it. In the end, organization is the way to determine work flows and relationships of people to maximize effectiveness while minimizing effort.

Remember, successful open groups evangelize unbelievers, enlist believers who are nonmembers, and enroll believers who are worship attendees but not in open groups. Once people are in a group, the strategy is to provide Bible teaching, fellowship, foundational discipleship, and ministry. It is unlikely that an open group will succeed if its organization does not mirror this strategy. Assigning people for each critical function is essential to a successful organization.

3. Train, Train, and Train!

Another key to successful open groups is to train every leader in your organization. Because we are so pressed for time today, many of our churches are failing at this critical point. I often see churches with good strategies and solid organizations. They are focused on reaching and teaching people and have a passion for what they are attempting to do, but training is lacking. If you don't train, you will have people doing their own thing, and you will never reach your strategy. I do not mean you must be autocratic, dictatorial, or heavy-handed. I do mean you must have organizational discipline to fulfill your strategy and reach your goals.

Everyone needs training whether it is at work, in sports, or in small groups. The level of teaching, evangelism, fellowship, and ministry you have in your groups is proportionally tied to training. Don't let the schedules of your people prevent you from training. You may not get to do all you want at first, but in time they will see the value of training. The success you see over time will be a result of those you train. Remember, you cannot do it all. This is a lay ministry, and your people must be trained for success. Do it weekly. Do it over a Web site. Do it periodically at retreats or conferences. Do it one-to-one in homes. But *do it!*

This is one area where you have many resources to help you. There is no end to training conferences, videos, books, and experts to help you have successful open groups. If you have Sunday

School, then you have help across the nation and literally around the world. Sunday School has been around since the nineteenth century, and it is as viable today as ever. But the same is true for cell groups, home fellowships, and the like. Just remember that training is best when it is basic. It is done in every venue, so why not in your church?

4. A Home of Their Own

You have a great strategy, a detailed organization, and a training plan. All is well and good so far, but a question remains. Where will these people meet? No matter how you choose to do your groups, they have to meet someplace. You are responsible for the time and location. If they are to meet in your church building, then rooms have to be dedicated and prepared for them. If they meet in homes, someone has to enlist members to open their homes and prepare for the group to meet. Time and place are crucial decisions because they lead to other issues. If you have open groups during the week in homes or at church, then you have to consider child care, times of meeting, and the length of the classes.

5. Go Get Them

You have a great strategy. You have a good understanding of what you want to accomplish and how you want it done. Now what is left? Go get them. That's right, in order to execute your strategy, you have to get some people to come to your open groups. How should you do it? In the best, most efficient way possible. Call them, visit them, E-mail them, or anything else that works. I can assure you that there are many people who can tell you what will not work, so let me tell you what will work. Whatever you work will work!

I smile as I think of the examples I am sharing with you here. I was in southern California listening to a radio interview of a famous researcher who said emphatically that you can no longer do confrontational evangelism and visit people in their homes. "The day of Sunday School and home visitation is over," he proclaimed. That night, within ten miles of this man's home, we conducted door-to-door visitation using three-person teams and led seventy-three people to faith in Christ! Don't let anyone tell you what works and what will not. Use anything you must, but go after people and get them in your open groups.

Let's review open groups before moving on. They are person-centered, lay-led, and Bible-based. They exist for evangelism, teaching, fellowship, and foundational discipleship. They are powerful partners with good worship services because both are occasions where believers and unbelievers participate together. In each, the five functions are present, helping a church fulfill the Great Commission and extend the kingdom of God. The church at worship becomes the church at work through successful open groups.

Chapter 12

MATURING BELIEVERS: CLOSED GROUPS

P ASTOR MIKE IS GETTING EXCITED as he begins to understand the
relationship of his small groups to the rest of his church's strategy.
His confidence rises as he imagines how his people are going to be
trained and equipped to minister. Making disciples, maturing them,
and multiplying them is simple enough to understand and not that
hard to do. But he needs to structure his closed groups to equip his
people for ministry. What exactly does this mean, and what does it
look like?

He remembers that only one year ago he and his leaders changed
his small-group curriculum to attract more people. It seemed to work
for three months, then attendance fell again, and so it was back to
square one. What is going to be different this time? Three simple
words: *be, know,* and *do.* These little words are the keys to the success
of closed groups.

*Closed groups exist to build kingdom leaders and to equip believers to
serve by engaging them in a way that moves them toward spiritual transformation through short-term, self-contained training in an atmosphere
of accountability to God and to one another.*

A Kingdom-Focused Church Model and Process

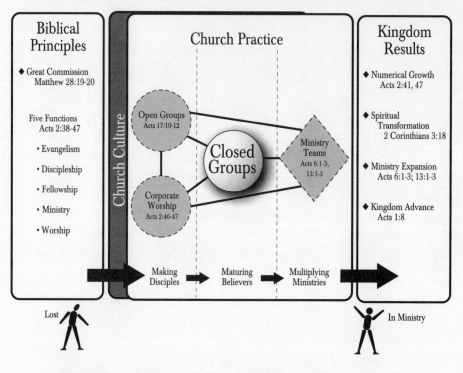

Remember, open groups exist to reach people and put them into relationships. A successful strategy for closed groups—still person-centered, lay-led, and Bible-based—equips them for kingdom ministry. And while the focus of closed groups begins at the same place as open groups, the experience is different in that they are generally more content-centered. Open groups begin small and grow. Closed groups generally begin large and finish with a smaller number at the end. Open groups are indefinite in length, while closed groups last for a specific period of time. Open groups are built to teach, evangelize, and assimilate. Closed groups are designed to equip leaders for ministry. Open groups reach unbelievers and believers alike. Closed groups focus on believers who need maturity for ministry.

Closed groups are incubators that begin with believers who are eager to learn how to put their faith into practice and share it with others. Closed groups exist to build kingdom leaders and equip them to be kingdom multipliers through short-term training and study. Open groups and the worship service are crafted to make everyone feel welcome, while closed groups are more intense, aimed at attaining a greater degree of biblical knowledge and familiarity with Christian concepts.

Closed groups represent the maturing stage that continues and intensifies the assimilation process for new believers and members. Each one is an equipping group made up mostly of believers. Its focus is training, its context is discipling, and its intent is to move its members on to the next level of Christian experience and commitment.

This process of maturing a Christian—the transformation from discipled to discipler—is the future of evangelism. I think the greatest threat to the church today is the loss of discipleship-building ministries where mature, spiritually transformed Christians can multiply themselves through other people. The Great Commission emphasizes both evangelism and discipleship.

In order for believers to minister effectively, they must be transformed in Christ (be), they must know the truth (know), and they must have the skills and/or spiritual gifts to minister effectively (do).

Closed groups are balanced between being/becoming, knowing, and doing. They must be designed to be comprehensive and continuous as we continually train disciples. If we train them well, then believers will manifest the three important characteristics of mature disciples—love, faith, and obedience—while at the same time effectively ministering in kingdom work.

Studies show that believers have six primary concerns for their lives. They want to grow personally in their relationship to Christ. They also want help with home and family, educating their children, understanding their world, their work, and their church. In other words, a believer wants to grow in Christ as an individual, a husband or wife, a parent, a citizen of the kingdom of God, and a citizen of the world, and they want to work in a vocation with kingdom meaning.

Stepping Stones

In order to meet these needs most effectively, believers must be taught and trained in seven critical areas. Curriculum for closed groups builds on seven foundational "stones" that are crucial for maturity. Each area or stone facilitates a believer's maturity in the three areas of being, knowing, and doing. Although they are listed below, they are not in sequence, nor are they finished with only one "course" or experience. These stones are comprehensive and continuous in our lives.

1. The principal focus should be the kingdom of God. The only way any person will ever be able to do anything in God's kingdom is by His grace and through His power.

2. Members need to come to a clear understanding of their identity in Christ. Believers become mature and overcome sin only when Christ becomes the focus of their lives.

3. As a believer's relationship with God changes, other relationships also are changed—home and family, work or school, and all other relationships as well.

4. Participants come to experience the church as the family of God and to understand that the body of Christ functions through gifts of the Spirit and relates to others out of the fruit of the Spirit.

5. Participants reevaluate their careers (or school) in light of scriptural truth. They explore the relationship of work and their calling as believers.

6. Believers face the reality of spiritual warfare in the world, arming themselves against temptation and Satan, praying in the power of God, and rejoicing to see people delivered from strongholds of evil.

7. Members develop a biblical worldview as they see how believers and churches can impact culture and society.

A Strategy for Closed Groups

What is the strategy then for successful closed groups? First, you have to make sure you know the needs of the people you seek to help mature in Christ. Design groups for the people to be enlisted. Don't merely enlist people for the groups you determine to conduct. Let me say that again. Closed groups are designed for the needs of the people! Can I put it another way? Closed groups are not designed and then people enlisted who may be interested! Discover the needs of individual believers and then design groups that will give them the understanding they need, skills for ministry, or a path to spiritual transformation.

Remember, *being, knowing,* and *doing* are your goals. Some group resources can accomplish all three, while others attempt only one or two. Choose your curriculum carefully, and any that does not mature believers in this way should *never* be used. Life is short, and needs are great. Equip for life and ministry, and you will always have success.

The best place to recruit believers is from your open groups. The next best place is from your worship services. It is fine to recruit believers from outside your church, but your primary obligation is to equip the people who come to your church. It is always best to recruit individually with a goal in mind of what a particular group will do for that person. If you only promote your groups to your congregation at large, you will miss the majority of those who need the greatest help.

Remember, closed groups have a specific purpose for a specific time. You can best equip your people if you go to them and tell them why you want them to be in the group you have designed. If they know what to expect, the length of the class, and the outcomes they will receive, then they are likely to come. It always depends on a believer's faithfulness, availability, and desire, but leaders can do a better job when everything is clearly planned and presented.

Design the groups for all levels of spiritual maturity: beginning, basic, advanced. Repeat groups throughout the year that meet the needs of large numbers of your people. Make them continuous, and make your curriculum comprehensive. There is never a time when a believer can stop learning, so keep at it.

Before we move on, I want to make an important statement concerning using closed-group curriculum for open groups. What I say may not seem profound, but I can assure you that what follows will save you time, distress, and keep you from failure. As I've already noted, open groups differ from closed groups in several ways. Differences in strategy, purpose, effects, and intensity mean the curriculum must be different as well. Open groups include believers and unbelievers, so there must be a curriculum that meets the needs of both groups. What curriculum can evangelize lost people and at the same time build believers? The Bible is the only answer to that question. The Bible is inspired and used by the Holy Spirit to convict and convert unbelievers, while at the same time transforming believers into Christlikeness. I urge you to keep open groups focused on Bible study that allows people to come in at any time. If you use a closed-group curriculum in an open group, the group will shut down quickly and lose its effectiveness.

Pastor Mike now sees the pattern Scripture presents as the successful way to do church. He realizes that there is a way to do what he has been called to do. Leadership, no matter how stressful, can only be done if the leader understands the what, how, and why of the task. Mike understands that God has called him to lead and equip his people to make disciples of unbelievers, to mature believers, and to equip them to minister. He knows that he is to multiply himself in the Great Commission task through his people.

Pastoring is never easy. Leading a church is often stressful. Kingdom work is sometimes a battle, but it is impossible without a kingdom focus. A kingdom focus points everyone to the Great Commission, the five church functions, and the map that describes the process we follow. It is logical, spiritual, and effective. It is not a method that is here today and gone tomorrow. It is not a means of adapting or copying someone else's successful strategy to your own situation. A kingdom focus links the how to the what and why of ministry. It influences the design of ministry as a whole and in its parts. It makes possible what is many times unknowable to pastors and church leaders.

Armed with this new insight, Pastor Mike is ready to begin the day. Confident of the outcome while mindful of the challenges, he is pleased to surrender himself to the Lord and His will for his church. He is eager to see what the Lord will do in, around, and through him and his people. He has a kingdom focus, a kingdom agenda, and a kingdom passion.

Chapter 13

MULTIPLYING MINISTRIES: MINISTRY TEAMS

A T LAST MIKE COMES TO THE GOAL of his kingdom-focused strategy—multiplying ministries. Armed with a fresh vision, his purpose now is to see every person evangelized, every believer built up into Christ and engaged in kingdom ministry.

This is the pattern we saw in Matthew 9, and it must be ours. Too many churches fail right here, but ministry is our ultimate goal for disciples.

We saw first corporate worship and open groups—welcoming, visitor-friendly, and open to all—with the purpose of forming new believers and making them disciples. Then we looked at closed groups—intense, tightly focused, primarily Christian activities that serve as incubators to transform disciples into kingdom multipliers. Ministry teams exist to build up the body of believers for service within the church and for missions throughout the world.

The diagram on the next page helps us get a clear picture of how each element of church practice fits into the process of moving the lost person (far left) to a position of ministry and service (far right). Notice how the worship and open-group circles have broken lines, reflecting the idea that anyone can enter at any time.

A Kingdom-Focused Church Model and Process

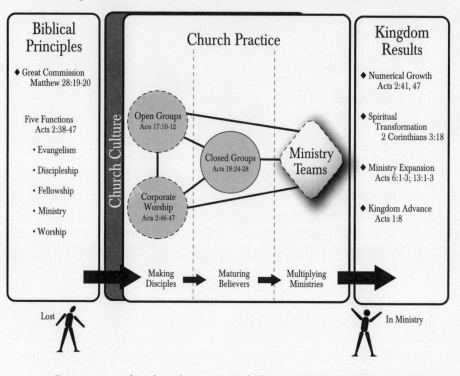

In contrast, the closed-group circle has a solid line, indicating that these groups are closed and self-contained for short periods of time.

The diamond—the subject of this chapter—is represented by broken lines. We will explain how ministry teams are open at any time. Notice how the lines joining each element of church practice run in both directions. This is a good picture of the dynamic process at work as we make disciples, mature believers, and multiply ministries in a local church setting.

Ministry teams exist to build up the body of Christ to accomplish the work of service within the church and to advance the kingdom of God throughout the world. The work of kingdom advance is a work of beginning new kingdom communities with an urgency to reach those without Christ.

150

Ministry teams represent the multiplying stage that lets members extend their reach and magnify their impact on the culture. Every Christian has the opportunity to lead many others to Christ, and each of those in turn can then carry the message to another, wider circle of people, geometrically increasing the number of people saved.

One of the most successful ministry team churches I know was developed by Charles Roesel, pastor of First Baptist Church, Leesburg, Florida. Like many established congregations in transitional neighborhoods, the Leesburg church faced the decision of whether to stay downtown or follow the population growth to the suburbs. They decided to stay. Pastor Roesel founded a great ministry on the example of Christ, showing us that evangelism is paramount. He and his church not only minister to the needy but also baptize them, train them, and send them out as evangelists. They see their success not in numbers or statistics but in faces.

The 1990s saw a dramatic rise in the use of short-term small groups designed to equip Christians for ministry. You would think there should also be a big increase in the ministry activities of individual Christians. But except for a few isolated instances, such as the rise in the number of short-term missions volunteers, no such increase occurred. On the contrary, research shows that many churches say one of the greatest challenges they face is getting enough people to serve in existing ministries, much less having enough to initiate new programs. These churches move ahead as well as they can, leaning heavily on a relatively small band of dedicated members who do it all. Burnout is alarmingly common.

In other words, there's a troubling disconnect between the rising number of closed-group studies and the stagnant percentage of participants actually going on to get involved in ministry. This underscores the importance of doing more than just training Christians. Church leaders must *inspire* them to *action*. Let's look at how ministry teams can greatly improve a church's prospects for success in raising up members to evangelize in Jesus' name.

Every denomination has congregations that are known for their attention and compassion in ministering to their members. Whatever the need—physical, emotional, or social—those churches are quick to meet it. Other congregations are known for evangelistic or social programs that concentrate on reaching people outside the church. The fact is that a successful kingdom-focused church has to have *both*.

Ministry teams appear throughout the Bible. From the moment Jesus sent the Twelve on their first assignment to the ministry of Paul and Silas, the Bible teaches that Christians are to join forces to proclaim the good news. Ministry teams of some sort are also part of virtually every church. The problem, which is the same problem we've seen in other places, is that teams too often lose sight of the need to share the gospel. Without this focus, they'll keep the church busy but accomplish very little.

Ministry teams that produce kingdom multipliers with the skills and conviction they need to win the lost to Christ share a number of similarities. First and most important, they have to filter out any goals or activities that are incompatible with fulfilling the Great Commission. Ministry teams have to be built on biblical principles and focused on biblical results.

Second, they must fulfill one or more of the five functions of a kingdom-focused church, which we identified in chapter 7 as evangelism, discipleship, fellowship, ministry, and worship.

And third, they should target specific kingdom results: numerical growth, spiritual transformation, ministry expansion, and kingdom advance.

Ministry teams can be focused in toward the congregation or out toward the community. Notice that the diamond on the diagram points both inward and outward. One shouldn't dominate the other.

There should be a place somewhere on a ministry team for every qualified person who wants to get involved. Every Christian is charged with being involved in ministry. Ministry teams also supply leadership to the other groups within a kingdom-focused church; corporate worship, open groups, and closed groups alike look to ministry teams to produce their leaders.

By now it shouldn't surprise you to learn there's no set structure for a successful ministry team. They're as varied as the churches themselves and the communities they serve. Their members might include church event planners, trustees, committee chairmen, ushers, deacons, benevolence-fund managers, teacher-training groups, broadcast-ministry managers, activity directors, and many others.

These teams prepare each member for what he or she is best gifted to do in carrying out the Great Commission. Paul wrote:

Christ did not send me to baptize, but to preach the gospel—not with clever words, so that the cross of Christ will not be emptied of its effect (1 Cor. 1:17).

So, what is Apollos? And what is Paul? They are servants through whom you believed, and each has the role the Lord has given. I planted, Apollos watered, but God gave the growth. So then neither the one who plants nor the one who waters is anything, but only God who gives the growth. Now the one who plants and the one who waters are equal, and each will receive his own reward according to his own labor. For we are God's co-workers. You are God's field, God's building (1 Cor. 3:5–9).

Principles for Ministry Teams

However they look on the outside and whatever their function, every well-running ministry team is supported by common key principles. The styling may be different, but under the hood the running gear is all the same.

1. Filtering

Every action must be filtered through the Great Commission, the five functions, and kingdom results. This filtering will ensure that everyone knows the direction and the intention of each ministry team. Mission statements for every ministry team will guide them to be focused on their overall mission.

2. Internal/External Focus

Churches need a balance between teams that serve within the church and teams that minister outside the church. Many churches have an overabundance of internal activities that can turn them inward. This will cut the church off from the needs around them. Some churches focus so heavily on mission and ministry actions outside the church that their leadership becomes weak and ineffective in the long run. The key is a healthy balance between inwardly focused ministry teams and outwardly focused ministry teams.

3. Universal Involvement

All believers are gifted for some responsibility in the ministry of the church. Helping them find their places of service helps the church and the kingdom. God gives each person gifts, talents, natural abilities, and interests for His glory. Involving each individual enables churches to build the body of Christ and reach out to a dying world.

4. Integration

All open groups, closed groups, and corporate worship activities are led and impacted by ministry teams. A system of teaching and training is critical to prepare new leaders for all the groups within the church. Well-planned ministry teams will provide support for each ministry area while finding and training new leadership.

5. Commission

Each ministry team functions under the authority of the church. Some churches have a formal plan for helping ministry teams be effective. Some churches have not thought about an integrated plan for the overall church. Each church should begin to seek ways to empower its members to live out the call of God in their lives.

We all have to commit ourselves to ministry in the power and authority of Christ. We can't waste precious time, energy, and resources on schemes that are contrary to God's plan. That plan is a basic one: We are commissioned to go under the authority of Christ to evangelize the world, baptize believers, and disciple them in Christlikeness. Anything we choose to do in ministry that fails to transform people by God's grace and equip them to minister with spiritual gifts is not a priority. In fact, I'll go so far as to say churches and believers who practice kingdom principles are the only ones who discover the ministries God intends for them.

Where is your church going to get all these leaders to steer it on a kingdom course? *Every* unsaved person is a potential convert to be won and baptized, and every one of them is a *potential minister of God.* The Lord seeks to save the lost and inspire them to be His ministers of reconciliation. This is the primary goal of every believer and every local church. Anything else is a departure from the gospel and the Great Commission. Don't be lured into sacrificing the best things for the good things.

How then can we change the life and culture of our churches to conform to God's will and work to join His mission to redeem our world? By keeping a kingdom focus.

Chapter 14

MODELS WITH A KINGDOM FOCUS

A LTHOUGH SUCCESSFUL CHURCHES are invariably kingdom-focused, there's a world of difference between one successful church and another in the way they worship, their size, music ministry, and lots of other variables that go into building the personality of the congregation. By describing the characteristics of a Great Commission church, I don't mean to limit what your church should do. As long as a church maintains its kingdom focus above any other objective and as long as it concentrates on transforming unbelievers into believers and from there into kingdom multipliers, it can—and should—do whatever else possible to serve its people and the community in the name of Christ.

Several types of churches have gotten a lot of attention in recent years because of their incredible rates of growth, with big conferences and best-selling books effectively publicizing their miraculous development. The place where these popular church models and the kingdom-focused church intersect is *absolutely crucial.*

There are two essential points to understand here. First, when you peel back the operational diagrams and checklists, all of these models are built around the same components of a kingdom focus we've explored in the last several chapters. They might not always call them the same thing or divide the process into the same steps, but the focus is there.

Second, except for the kingdom focus, the success of these models depends on variables that your church may or may not have. Some growth strategies favor big churches; some depend on a specific worship style; some will not transfer easily from one regional culture to another. While the kingdom focus aspect of these models is timeless and universally applicable, the processes are not.

In other words, be careful what you copy. And never get sidetracked from your church's ultimate goal.

Historically, church growth in America has been a reflection of population growth. The faster the population grew, the faster church attendance and membership grew. Traditional church programs such as Sunday School tended to be most successful when churches stayed theologically orthodox and when the laity had a close and mutually respectful relationship with the leaders.

It's interesting to note that, at least for Southern Baptists, the Great Depression of the 1930s was a high-water mark in the growth of the church. It is the only decade in the history of the denomination to record four million baptisms. Sunday School evangelism, Vacation Bible School, Training Union, and other programs brought hope to a generation devastated by the worst financial collapse in American history.

In the course of their development, these church programs went through similar life cycles. They began as cultural ideas or trends, transformed into parachurch movements, and then were assimilated into the church over time. When the leaders had a vision and a burden for a program, it thrived. When there were conflicts, or when the focus or ideology became blurred, the program plateaued or declined. Sometimes this process was relatively rapid, though more often it happened slowly over many years.

Sunday School, for example, was a fixture in evangelical societies for more than sixty years before it was officially embraced by the Southern Baptist Convention (SBC) in 1891. By 1900 about half of SBC congregations had a Sunday School program. After rapid growth during the first half of the twentieth century, Sunday School expansion has been in a holding pattern for a generation.

Surveys have had trouble pinpointing specific factors that determine whether a traditional program will succeed. A major reason is that church members who are hard at work making these programs happen are so absorbed in the immediate task that they don't stop to think about the goal or focus of what they're doing. They're busy preparing a lesson or cooking hamburgers or decorating a bulletin board because that's what they're supposed to do. They really haven't given the objective much thought.

To be worth the time and trouble, traditional church programs need a kingdom focus, and everybody in the loop has to understand what that means. Eighty-five percent of churches in a LifeWay Christian Resources survey claimed that the most important measure of success in discipleship ministry is how much lives are changed. However, church leaders report that 52 percent of adults involved in discipleship ministries at their churches experience little or no change in their Christian life and maturity, with only 21 percent experiencing major change.

To jump-start these underperforming traditional programs as well as the congregations themselves, a number of innovative church types have appeared on the scene in the last thirty years. Let's look at some of the best known in light of their kingdom focus and see what they can teach us.

One kind of church that's gotten lots of attention has been the "seeker-sensitive" church. The theory here is that people don't come to church because they're not comfortable there. They find traditional worship and programs irrelevant and unwelcoming. In response, these churches emphasize the social aspects of attendance, entertaining pop-style music, and practical, encouraging messages.

Certainly one of the best-known seeker-sensitive churches is Saddleback Community Church in California. Since its founding in 1979 with two families, Saddleback has grown to a membership of forty-five hundred with weekly attendance of more than fifteen thousand! Obviously they're doing something right. And what they're doing at the core is building a kingdom-focused church.

It's easy to think of Saddleback as a seeker-sensitive church, and a cursory reading of pastor Rick Warren's exciting book about Saddleback, *The Purpose Driven Church,* can reinforce that assumption. But here's an important point to notice. At the center of Saddleback's Five Circles of Commitment, Twelve Convictions About Worship, and other program processes are the essentials of a kingdom focus.

Their development process of commitment to "Membership, Maturity, Ministry, and Missions" accurately traces the same journey we've identified from unbeliever to believer to kingdom multiplier. Their affirmation that a "service geared toward seekers is meant to supplement personal evangelism not replace it" expresses their recognition of the supreme importance of evangelizing. This recognition is reinforced by Saddleback's stated goal of bringing glory to God "by presenting Jesus Christ with as many Christlike disciples as we possibly can before he returns" in keeping with Colossians 1:28: "We proclaim Him, warning and teaching everyone with all wisdom, so that we may present everyone mature in Christ."

Characteristics of a prominent seeker-sensitive church may be transplantable to your congregation or they may not. It would be a mistake to try to grow your church by turning it into a carbon copy of Saddleback—which, by the way, Rick Warren will be the first to tell you! How is your local culture different from southern California's? And what about neighborhood economics? Congregational traditions? The depth and dedication of lay leadership? The importance of buildings or a building program (which is relatively unimportant at Saddleback)? All these things that are tangential to a kingdom focus are subject to change. They have to be considered and adjusted to fit the specific needs of the people God has given you to reach.

An even more dramatic departure from traditional models is the "seeker-centered" church. Churches such as Willow Creek in suburban Chicago have built dynamic and influential ministries specifically targeting non-Christians. And, as with seeker-sensitive churches, the core characteristics—the ones that can be modeled most successfully by the widest range of congregations—are directly related to a kingdom focus.

A leader among seeker-centered churches, Willow Creek has developed Five G's considered necessary in followers of Christ, Ten Core Values, and a Seven-Step Strategy for Reaching the Lost. But their ultimate goal, as explained in the church's monthly magazine, is "to further His kingdom in our midst, but we also, in obedience to the Great Commission, labor to extend His kingdom worldwide."

A kingdom focus.

Since 1975, Willow Creek has gone from 125 participants a week to more than 17,000; over half of these are seekers. More than 5,600 churches have adopted Willow Creek principles and practices. In its outreach and training materials, Willow Creek is careful to explain that they don't claim their processes and philosophies are the best, but rather "no more or less than a pragmatic approach that works." They wisely point out that the details may not be right for you. You can't photocopy the Willow Creek program and start it in your church Monday morning unless all the variables line up, as well. What you can do is learn how, building on a kingdom focus, they have built an incredibly powerful and successful ministry with *their* leadership in *their* community using the gifts and talents *they* had available at the time.

A third, distinctive kind of church is the "cell church," consisting of many small cells of five to fifteen worshipers under the leadership of one pastor. The cells combine for congregational meetings at regular intervals, but the emphasis is on the cells. It's a church *of* small groups instead of a church *with* small groups. Cell churches have a compassion for the lost and unchurched, a focus on multiplication of cells and new churches, and a desire to be Great Commission Christians by being ready to minister at every opportunity.

Christ designed His church to thrive in its most basic life form. This is as true for us today as it was for first-century Christians. The simplest, most resilient building block of life is the cell; it's also the most basic and vital building block of the church. Dr. Ralph Neighbour observes that "cells exist to fulfill the Great Commission of making disciples of every nation."

When Bob Russell began his work as pastor of Southeast Christian Church in Louisville, Kentucky, it was a small, traditional congregation. Russell based his ministry on preaching the Word of God and creating a fellowship of people to reach others. As a result, the membership formed cells to study the Word and encourage others, so that before long there were four to five thousand people meeting in cells every week. On weekends the total number of people at worship is nearly twenty thousand!

Though cell churches are some of the largest churches in the world, Neighbour warns of the danger of focusing on the wrong goal: "Cells developed to make a church grow will fail every time. Growth is never the goal; it is the natural by-product of doing something right."

Depending on the needs of the participants, cells might emphasize testimonies or Bible study or prayer or any of a combination of other programs. They do what they need to do to bring that body of believers and seekers into the service of Christ.

Whatever the method, the outcome is the same: evangelism. Cell-group leaders aren't necessarily teachers, but they are always people who can care for and nurture others. Their success depends on their ability to transfer their commitment to evangelism to the rest of the cell. We are all called to serve, and one of the best ways for a young Christian to get a foothold on the ladder of leadership is to care for another member of the cell, encouraging and entrusting that person with values to pass on to others. It's the cell version of building kingdom multipliers.

A kingdom focus.

By the time they reach a position of cell leadership, members have been shown to exhibit exceptional enthusiasm, dedication, and spirituality. Cells also have apprentice leaders who will eventually start new cells of their own.

Here again the particulars might be different from what you're used to, but cell churches have been a valuable tool for the kingdom. Some of the largest churches in the world are cell churches in Korea, including the world's largest Methodist congregation and the two largest Presbyterian churches.

Bethany World Prayer Center in Baton Rouge, Louisiana, has established cell groups all over town. Pastor Larry Stockstill explains that the cell version of kingdom multipliers is developing leadership for new cells. They use the FAITH strategy to build a cell church, and they do it successfully. I know this for a fact because I have a spy in the system. My aunt is a member there.

God has used cell churches in a mighty way. It's a type of church that has been successful under some circumstances—where there are lots of lay leaders, high population density, and pastors who aren't prone to be personal empire builders. It could be a good type for your church—if the variables are right—and if a kingdom focus comes before anything else.

You get the idea.

In 1982, Bobby Welch, pastor of First Baptist Church in Daytona Beach, Florida, and Doug Williams, the minister of evangelism, decided to focus the energy and resources of their church on evangelism training. Three years later they combined the evangelism ministry with Sunday School. This produced a powerful outreach effort that used the familiar Sunday School framework to spread the gospel with new levels of dedication, training, and resolve.

It was Sunday School with afterburners, and it worked. Tried-and-true Sunday School became a launching pad for meaningful, deeply engaging evangelism outreach. The kingdom gained new converts, and First Baptist Daytona grew dramatically both in size and influence as its members evangelized, then trained new Christians to be evangelists themselves.

Several years later this strategy combining evangelism and Sunday School was given the acronym FAITH to help train believers in the process of nurturing and strengthening their faith. It then was made available to other churches.[1] Since that time thousands of church members have been equipped by FAITH to refresh and encourage pastors and congregations across the country, establish a kingdom focus, and increase Sunday School attendance, church enrollment, and baptisms.

FAITH intersects with every stage of evangelism—worship, open groups, closed groups, and ministry teams—but Sunday School is at its heart.

FAITH has brought a new kingdom focus and new success to many other churches. In one church average Sunday School attendance has skyrocketed from 90 to 150, with a high of 200. The pastor there calls FAITH "an equipping ministry." He adds, "It is something we can use consistently and claim as our own. As a result we have grown. God has consistently added to our church. Members have the potential to do more than they ever thought possible." The church body is more diverse than ever before, but there's "no contention between older members and newer, younger adults. Instead, there is a sweet spirit as the older pillars are excited to see the work they have begun being continued by younger members."

The best way to describe the meteoric growth of Fellowship Church is "it's a God thing." That's the way pastor Ed Young and the rest of the staff describe what is taking place in the thousands of lives across the Dallas-Fort Worth Metroplex.

Fellowship Church started as an extension of an existing church in Irving, Texas. A committed group of families determined to plant a church in the northern part of the city. Ed Young became the church's first pastor in February 1990. He focused the mission of the church to reach out to the unchurched community.

The church moved from an office location to the 750-seat Irving Arts Center in its first year of existence. While in this location the church grew from a few hundred to more than three thousand attendees. In 1994, the church began to look for a site to build a permanent location, settling in Grapevine about three miles north of the Dallas-Forth Worth Airport.

In October 1996, the church moved to MacArthur High School. During the next eighteen months, the church grew to five thousand people attending each weekend. Fellowship Church moved into its current 125,000-square-foot location on April 5, 1998. More than seven thousand people attended the first weekend.

Today more than sixteen thousand people attend the church each weekend. Fellowship Church's HomeTeams ministry, designed to build a network of small groups within the context of the larger community, develops authentic and lasting relationships within Fellowship. Power Source, the educational program, offers a wide variety of age-appropriate classes with practical teaching and life application to help members learn and unleash God's limitless power in their lives.

The purpose statement of the church is balanced among three biblical mandates for the local church. Fellowship Church exists to reach up, reach out, and reach in. Every program, budget request, and idea is filtered through the purpose statement.

Reaching up means worshiping God. The only way believers can express true love to God and worship Him is through a personal relationship with Jesus Christ. Fellowship calls that person a Christ follower.

Another key purpose of Fellowship is to reach out to people who do not attend a local church. Fellowship people invite their friends, family, neighbors, and coworkers to attend so that they will hear and understand what it means to be a follower of Jesus Christ.

The church reaches in to help believers grow in their spiritual maturity and become fully developed followers of Christ. Because the Christian life is one of constant growth and development, Fellowship Church focuses on providing biblical principles that can be applied to everyday life.

Never underestimate the power of a kingdom focus.

Chapter 15

Reaching Your Compelling Image of an Achievable Future

WE HAVE FOLLOWED YOUNG PASTOR MIKE through a journey of discovery and effectiveness. He has learned that asking the right questions leads to the right answers, which in turn leads to the right applications. He has taken steps to apply what he learns, and he will do fine.

Pastor Mike is fictional. He doesn't exist, but you and I do. What leaders do in response to the call of God on our lives and His commissioning us to serve His churches is the most important thing we have to do in our lives.

How we lead and what we accomplish literally means spiritual life and death to millions of people on earth. Our resolve to lead churches in making disciples, maturing them, and putting them into kingdom ministries is the central focus of our lives because it is the central focus of the kingdom of God. Nothing is more important than our correct response to His call and agenda.

You and I can get and stay busy on a million things under the umbrella of ministry. But if we never get a kingdom focus, if we never make disciples and mature them, if we never extend our ministries through the lives of our people, we will ultimately fail. It is time to get off the merry-go-round of ministry and onto the kingdom-multiplying road. It is time to stop what is not important and start what is. It is time to take a risk, make the changes, and move on toward fulfilling our calling and ministry.

If our churches were all healthy and strong, we would not need to be so concerned with making changes and taking drastic steps. If churches were growing and healthy, you would not be reading this book, and I would not have written it! I challenge you to examine your life and ministry to see if you have a passion for the kingdom of God and its Great Commission. I urge you to take an honest look at how you feel about your people and your church to see if you have multiplied yourself in their lives and sent them on ministry. Stay with them; lead them to a kingdom focus. Some of your folks are ready right now to follow your leadership into a kingdom focus and are eager to join you in the work.

So where are you going from here? I wish we could spend a few hours together and talk about the how, what, where, why, and when of all the things in this book. I would enjoy hearing your questions and asking some of my own. I have never found time with a pastor wasted or boring. You live in an intersection of life that few leaders will ever know about and even fewer can see. You live where life happens and where people are transformed by the power of God. You live in a swirl of disappointment, sin, salvation, joy, grief, power, worship, and transformation. And that is just a normal day for you! If we were not called by a sovereign God to do what we do, then our problems would quickly burn us up and leave us ruined.

Aren't you glad that He is ultimately responsible for whatever happens? God is large enough to know everything, powerful enough to keep things together, and gracious enough to help us get through each day. Today you may feel the pressure and grind of serving Him, but tomorrow you will know the gladness of His working through you to accomplish His purposes. I just wish we had some downtime together to talk about it more.

If this book has any lasting benefit for you, I hope it at least includes a fresh look at the kingdom of God. Trust me, your understanding of the kingdom is going to make the difference in your future leadership and effectiveness. The more you know of the kingdom, the better able you are to understand what is happening in our world and what God is doing in it. The kingdom of God is the ultimate reality for knowing God and experiencing Him fully. Test everything you do by whether it helps your church fulfill the Great Commission. If it does, pursue it; if it doesn't, find a way to get rid of it. I know this is easier said than done. It is always easier to add something in a church than to take something away. But of course, that is part of the problem, isn't it? We keep adding and adding while never eliminating. Take your time but move deliberately to minimize anything that hurts kingdom work. I would like to offer you a few suggestions to help you lead your church successfully.

Be the leader you are. That may sound trite, but if you think about it for a moment, it makes sense. Do not try to be anyone else or to do what others do. I regret that many leadership resources suggest that most leaders struggle because something is wrong with them. It may not be stated so boldly, but in reality the prospects of who you are at present are generally discounted by these resources as they promise great success with a "leadership makeover." Listen, God made you who you are with a plan and intention concerning what He would do through you.

Never quit learning or being transformed by Christ. But this in no way means you have to become somebody else in order to lead well. Before the world was created, God determined to create you and to bring you into a dynamic relationship with Himself. He provided satisfaction and remedy for all your sinful choices, including your salvation through Christ. He determined to call you into His service in order to work through you to accomplish a part of His kingdom plan. He gave you the gift of life and gifts for living and service. You are equipped and able to grow into the ministry He has for you. You are His vessel, and you need not worry about what others are doing in His work. Do whatever the Lord gives you, and do it with excellence.

Much of what you need to lead you already possess. Remember how you helped your children tie their shoes? They learned because you have ability to teach them, and they have an intuitive sense to learn. Everything you need to teach your people and everything they need to learn for ministry is already in place. Your innate ability to teach, communicate, and lead is in place. Their intuitive sense for kingdom, church, and spiritual things is already in place. The Holy Spirit will empower you to lead and empower them to understand.

I would not discount the difficulty of change for your people. However, I would not surrender for a moment the idea that people cannot and will not change simply because they haven't. Lead your people in your own way, but lead them!

Come to a full understanding of the foundation of a kingdom-focused church. This book is a start, and there are other resources to help you, but you must own this as a leader. You must be willing to study Scripture and pray over these important things. You must understand the nature of the kingdom of God and the nature of the church. These two things are nonnegotiable and must be accepted, understood, and applied, or you will never succeed in fulfilling your ministry.

Think with me about the five church functions and the four results. Examine again the full implications of the Great Commission for yourself and your church. Be honest in evaluating whether your church makes disciples, matures believers, and multiplies ministries. Don't ever evaluate your effectiveness by your activities. Look at results, but look at the right ones. Look at the number of people your church is leading to Christ. Account for the number of believers who are being spiritually transformed. Remember, spiritual transformation is *God's work* of changing a believer into the likeness of Christ by creating a new identity in Him and empowering a lifelong relationship of love, trust, and obedience. How many of your folks are truly experiencing this? Also, take note of the number of people you can reproduce yourself in and place them into various ministries. If you are still doing their work, then you are not leading successfully.

I suggest that you use the MAP to evaluate your ministry and that of your church. Where you are doing well, thank God for it and tell your people. Where you are not, begin to address the issues honestly and move to overcome them. Set your focus and help your church set its focus on aligning what you do with what the Bible says is right for a local church.

Never fear methods, old ones or new ones. Use what you have that works, and go get whatever else you need. Do not be afraid to try anything new, and don't be afraid to use old methods that work. Methods are tools, and old ones often work just as well or better than new ones. Let them serve your purposes for as long as they are helpful. Almost everything under the sun has been imagined, tried, and proven, so don't be afraid to get the help you need. Just remember that old things are not always bad things.

Get a group in your church together to talk about these things. Study Scripture together and pray. Stay before the Lord until He gives you the compelling image of your achievable future. Don't start with a formal group. Get someone to open his or her home, bring a cake, make some coffee, and have some cold drinks. Don't dominate the discussion and conversations, even though you might know more than anyone else.

Take your time and let them find their way to the changes you think might be helpful. Let the Lord guide everyone into the image of the future that is most exciting and achievable. Stay with them and be patient. Don't worry if things do not come around quickly.

If you lead your people well, I can tell you good things will follow. Where you are headed as a church is important. How you get there and how long it takes is also important but not as important. I've spent a lot of time in these pages describing how Great Commission churches work, but these ideas aren't my prescription for your church's success. The practices I have seen and experienced for the past thirty years as a church leader have worked because they produce kingdom-focused churches with kingdom-focused people. They work because they are biblical.

I wish I could claim that in every case everyone I pastored and led came through with me. I can't, and they didn't—but many did. I know that a kingdom-focused church will have the Great Commission as its one driving force for everything it does. I know this kind of church rests on the foundation of evangelism, discipleship, fellowship, ministry, and worship. Any church without all of these functions functioning will always be dysfunctional! I can promise you with all my honor that these functions will bring numerical growth and spiritual transformation. They also will bring ministry expansion and kingdom advance through missions.

It is entirely possible that as you build a kingdom-focused church, you will come up with new insights and methods that work better. If you do, that's great. It means that the core message of this book is right and you have broken through to effective, creative, and unique leadership. And since your ideas are your own, it will be time for you to write the next book on how to do church. I pray this is exactly what happens to you. The body of Christ needs help, and we are always ready for the latest insights and resources.

You may be tempted to look for shortcuts in building a kingdom-focused church. It is a common temptation, and if you find any, write me, because I'm still looking for some. Pastoring a church is somewhat like farming. Farming is a slow, deliberate affair. It is as unpredictable as the weather, and it requires patience and hard work. Successful farmers do not give up after one year of drought or flooding. Farming is a long process over many years, requiring a lifetime commitment for success.

Pastoring has many parallels to farming. You can't rush people any more than you can control their thoughts or behaviors. You have to teach and lead them patiently. You have to commit to their lives for a long time. You can't quit when things go bad or expect the good times to last forever. You have to balance out your work and keep a reign on emotional swings. You have to lead, but you can only lead by knowing where you are going and how to get there.

Some churches grow numerically more quickly than others. In some, believers are spiritually transformed before other results follow. Growth comes as the Lord reigns in the lives of individual believers and the congregation as a whole. Growth actually begins in a right relationship with God. Every approach to applying these principles is based on a personal relationship with Him.

The Lord speaks to His children in many ways. We get our directions from Him about what He is doing and what He wants done in our communities and churches to reach people for Christ. He speaks to us through the Holy Spirit, through prayer, through the Word, through others, and through our circumstances to show us what He is doing. Church work and church growth are God's work, so we can only be effective when we are in a right relationship with Him. Jesus said His work was the work of the One who sent Him (John 4:34). If Christ understood that His work belonged to the Father, we can do no less. We must seek the Father's presence and seek to do His will.

I know it may be difficult for you right now. You may be struggling, and you may feel unappreciated or unnoticed for all you do. You may have been hurt or wounded by something that has happened. You may look around and see no hope and no way out. I do not discount those feelings, but I want to say that our feelings are seldom the best indicator of reality.

Do you remember the story I told earlier about the church I pastored where the little girl was raped on our church bus near my house? I have never had a worse time than that anywhere I ever served. I remember thinking, *Lord, I'm ready for something else where I won't see these kinds of things, and my family won't be at such risk.*

What I was really saying to the Lord was that I wanted a nice, safe, successful, prosperous church somewhere else. I know now how wrong those feelings were. In fact, as I write these words, my eyes fill with tears at the remembrance of how selfish I was. During that time I awoke one night and couldn't sleep. I went to our den, and the Lord began to speak to me. He said, "Gene, you would really like to leave here, would you not?" "Yes," I replied, "I'm ready to go anywhere else." "You don't love these people, do you? In fact, you are afraid of them," He said. "That's right, Lord. I just want to leave."

What I heard next made me ashamed of myself. The Lord said to me, "The difference between Me and you, then, is that I love all the people here. I made them, and I sent you here to tell them and to show My love for them. If you leave, who will do that? I want *you* to do it."

I did not need another church. I needed a new heart and a kingdom focus. I needed an understanding of how God works in all places with all sorts of people to accomplish His will. So my encouragement to you is this. Don't spend all your time and energy looking for a way out. Get a kingdom focus and start living at your fullest capacity in the church where you now serve. God loves you, and He loves your people. He sent you there (yes, even to your difficult assignment) to work His purposes through you and into your people.

We desperately need pastors and church leaders who understand what a church is and who are willing to work to see that their churches become what God desires: churches with a kingdom focus above everything else. When the church you want is the church God wants, great things begin to happen. A kingdom-focused church is one that is simple, streamlined, and exciting. If you begin right now to take a few leaders with you toward a kingdom focus, then you will eventually see the results that you now label as potential.

Do you remember how Jesus built His disciples into kingdom warriors? He did it methodically, the same way my mentor, Dr. Tommy Lea, did it for me years ago. I was a college student, and Tommy pastored my home church. Liberty Baptist Church in Appomattox, Virginia, is a solid church with a rich heritage. One Sunday evening after church, Tommy asked me to read the book *The Master Plan of Evangelism* by Robert Coleman. He indicated that we would meet again to discuss it. I read the book, and we met for two weeks to discuss evangelism and my responsibility as a believer to share my faith. Following the second week, he told me about an evangelism training program called Evangelism Explosion. He explained how it worked and invited me to join him to learn how to do it. You are probably familiar with the approach, so I'll get to the point quickly.

At first, while I learned the details of the gospel presentation, I went visiting with Tommy and watched as he shared Christ. Later I shared a portion of the outline, and he shared the rest. Soon I was sharing the outline as Tommy observed. The pattern is clear, and it is the same pattern Christ used to build His disciples into kingdom agents. First, Tommy taught me about evangelism. Next he took me with him, and I watched as he shared Christ with people. Then we did it together as a team. Later I shared the presentation as he watched. Finally, I was able to share it on my own and take another person with me.

I realized later that Tommy was doing what Jesus did during His earthly ministry. He made disciples by calling them to follow Him. He matured them by teaching and training them the same way I was trained. Finally, He multiplied Himself through them, and they were able to do what He had done. In fact, to me the most staggering promise in the entire New Testament is John 14:12 where Jesus says, "'I assure you: The one who believes in Me will also do the works that I do. And he will do even greater works than these, because I am going to the Father.'" Jesus was multiplying Himself in His disciples to accomplish more.

A kingdom focus will give you the ability to make disciples through evangelism, using small groups, worship, special events, and other approaches. You will mature those you lead to Christ through small groups, worship, fellowship, and ministry. But you will move your people into kingdom work as you multiply yourself through them to the ministries God has in mind. You have a calling and a work. So do your people, and a kingdom focus releases both you and them to do it.

As I travel around our planet, I have the good fortune to meet believers in every imaginable context. Everywhere I go people want to know why they are here on earth and what God wants them to do in His kingdom. Often we answer those questions by getting them into groups and studies that give information but provide no transformation. We study and study, but we fail to raise up Christians to minister in the kingdom. We need to know the truth, and we need maturity. But also we and our people need to be equipped and sent out into the world to advance the kingdom of God. Getting people into kingdom work does not take long, or certainly not as long as we take. I think sometimes we worry about doctrinal and denominational purity and have little concern about kingdom obedience. Doctrine is crucial, but it cannot replace a focus on the kingdom of God and a passion to see people won to Christ and transformed into His likeness. Besides, witnessing believers aren't the source of our doctrinal problems. Their doctrine is right because it is in the center of the Great Commission.

I make no apologies for these statements, especially when I look around and see how many of our pastors are struggling as they lead struggling churches. If you are doing well, you probably don't need a book with an exhortation like this, but many of us need it, and we need it badly. We need a kingdom focus to help ourselves as leaders and our people as servants to do what God wants done in this generation. We must raise our sights and standards now, and with them we must raise our expectations. We have accommodated our culture long enough, and we have focused on those who do the least. Let's refocus on those who will do the most—the saints of God who are ready to move and ready for transformation and to be equipped for ministry. Let's focus on how to get as much of the kingdom of God into them and as much of them into the kingdom as possible in the shortest amount of time.

You may feel as Moses felt in the desert—alone, struggling, useless, and in need of direction and assurance. Your sheep may be worth as much as his were as they followed him around looking for pasture and water. You remember what happened, don't you? When God began to move in his life, He gave him a picture of the future that was so great Moses feared for his life! He never could have imagined or dreamed what God had in mind for him and the Israelites. I think the same is true for you today. God has a will and a plan for you and your church. You are not chained to a determined agenda that will keep you and your folks from doing what God wants done any more than the Israelites were hopelessly and forever in bondage to the pharaoh in Egypt. They, like Moses, could not see what God had determined to do.

What made the difference for Moses? First he had a fresh encounter with God, and he heard for himself what the Lord was about to do. Next he understood that God was going to use him to do something unthinkable, something great, and something that would change the history of the world. Often hidden in the dramatic events of the Exodus are the words of God, that put everything into focus. They are recorded in Exodus 19:1–6. Verses 4–6 provide the key to understanding all that God was doing:

> You yourselves have seen what I did to Egypt, and
> how I carried you on eagles' wings and brought you to
> myself. Now if you obey me fully and keep my covenant,
> then out of all nations you will be my treasured posses-
> sion. Although the whole earth is mine, you will be for
> me a kingdom of priests and a holy nation (NIV).

That is incredible! From the beginning the Lord wanted a people for Himself. They would be His kingdom, priests unto Him, and a people for Him among all the earth. Everything He did was for them and for this reason: He made them into a kingdom, His kingdom; and He gave them a kingdom focus.

It should be clear to you by now that the kingdom of God is the reign of God over all things in the universe. It is God's personal presence in and over all things. It comes to us by revelation, the greatest expression of which is seen in Jesus Christ. He is vitally connected to our lives and wants us to know Him and to be with Him forever. The kingdom of God is the message and reality Jesus brought to earth to give us peace and security forever. It is what every person in the world longs for and every person can have in knowing Christ as Lord. It was the desire of Greek philosophy, Roman rule, and the Hebrew religion. The wisdom of God is Jesus, the rule of God is Jesus Christ the Lord, and the worship of God is through Jesus Christ our Lord.

Mike discovered a compelling image for his church. A compelling image is essential. Nobody wants to pursue a boring image. But Mike also discovered an image of an achievable future. An achievable image adds credibility to the vision for the future; otherwise, all you get is a spiritual pipe dream. Combine the two—compelling and achievable—and you have what is required. That's what Mike always longed for. And he found it in the kingdom-focused church.

We end this book with the truth of the kingdom of God in Christ and our call to it. Called by a King, we are sent by Him to establish His kingdom in the lives of men and women, boys and girls, one person at a time. One by one, as we win them and equip them and send them, we establish His kingdom.

It is not likely that I have said much in this book that is new to you. But I hope I have given you truth and encouragement to focus your life, your ministry, your church and its people on the kingdom of God. You will never go wrong with a kingdom focus. None of us are excused from hardship and trials, but no one has to remain where he is. You can break out, and so can your church.

My prayer is that you and your church will move out in faith with the assurance of God's power and promise to use you to fulfill His Great Commission and to establish His kingdom in the lives of multitudes through Jesus Christ our Lord.

> Now may the God of peace, who brought up from
> the dead our Lord Jesus—the great Shepherd of the
> sheep—with the blood of the everlasting covenant, equip
> you with all that is good to do His will, working in us
> what is pleasing in His sight, through Jesus Christ, to
> whom be glory forever and ever. Amen. (Heb. 13:20–21).

May God bless you and your work. I hope to see you in the harvest fields sometime soon.

ENDNOTES

Chapter 3

1. John Kramp, *Getting Ahead by Staying Behind* (Nashville: Broadman & Holman Publishers, 1997), 4, 21.

Chapter 5

1. Gene Mims, *Thine Is the Kingdom* (Nashville: LifeWay Press, 1997), 11.
2. Dallas Willard, *Renovation of the Heart* (Colorado Springs: NavPress, 2002), 23.

Chapter 6

1. Augustus H. Strong, *Systematic Theology,* (Philadelphia: American Baptist Publication Society, 1909), 3:890.
2. Gene Mims, *The 7 Churches NOT in the Book of Revelation* (Nashville: Broadman & Holman Publishers, 2001).

Chapter 9

1. Gene Mims, *Kingdom Principles for Church Growth* (Nashville: Convention Press, 1994).

2. Rick Warren, *The Purpose Driven Church: Growth Without Compromising Your Message & Mission* (Grand Rapids: Zondervan, 1995).

Chapter 11

1. The five basic principles are adapted from Arthur Flake's five-step formula for building a Sunday School: discover the possibilities, enlarge the organization, provide the place, train the workers, and visit prospects.

Chapter 14

1. FAITH is based on the acronym from the witnessing plan: Forgiveness, Available, Impossible, Turn, Heaven. The FAITH strategty is the marriage of Sunday School with evangelism. For more information about FAITH, visit http://www.lifeway.com/sundayschool/faith/.